6 x 6/16 LT 5/16

Emily

Emily Smucker

Health Communications, Inc.
Deerfield Beach, Florida

www.hcibooks.com

Library of Congress Cataloging-in-Publication Data

Smucker, Emily.
    Emily / by Emily Smucker.
      p. cm.
    ISBN-13: 978-0-7573-1414-8
    ISBN-10: 0-7573-1414-7
    1. Smucker, Emily—Health.   2. Allergy in children—Patients—
Biography.   3. Mennonite children—Biography.   I. Title.
RJ386.S645 2009
362.198'92970092—dc22
  [B]

2009015386

Publisher: Health Communications, Inc.
          3201 S.W. 15th Street
          Deerfield Beach, FL 33442–8190

Cover photo ©BananaStock
Cover design by Larissa Hise Henoch
Interior design and formatting by Lawna Patterson Oldfield

To my mom, for loving me and feeling sorry for me and bringing me tea in bed even after I'd been sick for over a year.

Three Wishes

IF YOU HAD THE CHANCE to have three wishes (no wishing for more wishes), what would they be and why?

Okay, I admit, it would be easy to think of three easy answers:

1. That I would never get sick again.
2. That I would never get homework in the coming school year.
3. A nicer video camera.

It's also quite easy to get whatever your heart desires in three wishes, despite the whole "no wishing for more wishes" deal. You could wish:

1. That there would be no more suffering.

2. That whatever we wanted would appear like magic at the snap of our fingers.

3. That everyone would live happily ever after.

See? You could get everything in three wishes.

Oh, whatever. So I think the question is dumb. Who ever listens to me anyway? Maybe I'd better go take my temperature to see if it's gone down a fraction of an inch yet, and go lie in bed where I belong.

A Feeling

I'VE BEEN HAVING ANNOYING stomachaches lately. Sunday evening I had another one. So I sat out the whole church service, sipping tea and reciting Isaiah 40 to myself. I always recite Isaiah 40 to myself when I have stomachaches. It is very comforting.

I felt better by the time the service was over. My siblings and I went to our cousins Justin and Stephy's house, where we played soccer, ate food, and then just sat around while the guys played a game. It was during that time I began to know I was probably getting sick, because there is a certain feeling you get when you are getting sick. It's not just headache and sore throat—it's a sort of woozy feeling.

When we finally got home, which took a long time due to

my brother Matt's game playing, I took my temperature and had a sky-high fever.

Arg zarg. I don't want to be sick again. How will this affect my plans?

At least it's happening now, and not during school.

Plans

WE WERE HAVING A NORMAL youth function at my church—sitting around, talking, and having fun. We were mostly talking about what to do for a fundraiser. Should we do another slave auction, where kids from the youth group get auctioned off as slaves and have to do their owner's bidding for the day (within reason, of course)? That was the only idea anyone threw out, even though no one seemed to like it very much.

Then Phebe said, "I think Emily should write a play for us to perform."

A murmur of approval and a nodding of heads swept through the room. I glowed. A play! Could I actually write a play? I've written skits before. Actually, I usually just make them up and tell people what to do so I don't have to bother with scripts. But could I write a whole play?

"Okay, I'll do it," I said.

I'm gonna write a play! And the youth group is gonna perform it!

Wow, I have so many things planned for this year. I want to take college algebra at the community college, because I don't think I'm smart enough for advanced math, but I want to take *some* math this year. Plus, then I'll get some, you know, college experience.

I also want to get a job, because I can *finally* drive. And I'm going to be a senior, and at my school, that means I don't have to be in school full time. Oh yeah, and there is the little fact that I need money.

Somewhere, Mom found out about some community writing classes, and I think it would be so much fun to take one with her.

Oh, and now that I can drive, I can finally see if I can find some community theater or something to participate in. I'm tired of knowing nothing about drama other than what I make up.

This year I'm also probably going to be yearbook editor. I mean, Justin and I are the only ones who even know how to put pages together, and he was editor last year.

And now, this play! I'll probably have to direct it too, because who besides me can direct a play? Well, J. D. can, but I don't think he would really want to direct *my* play. I'll probably be put in charge of costumes too. I can't wait!

Wow. Yes, I know that is a lot. I'll probably have to drop something. Or several things. Still, I am looking forward to being *busy* for once.

Now I just need to get over this dumb sickness and *get started!*

Change

WELL, WELL, WELL. I am better I guess. Or at least, well enough to be doing things again, which pretty much translates into better.

And tomorrow is school. The summer is over. But what will the school year bring? It's my last year. Do you know what this means? Everything is changing, changing.

Sometimes it seems like things will always be the same, especially my family. My brother Matt will always talk about leaving the church, moving out, and getting a girlfriend, but never do any of them. He'll always be short on cash. And everyone will laugh when he says crazy stuff.

My sister Amy will keep going cool places and meeting cool people. She'll joke about getting a boyfriend but never actually get one. And she'll always come home.

Ben will always hate girls and love sports.

Steven will keep on doing silly stuff and make everybody laugh.

Jenny will be cute and get on my nerves.

Forever and ever.

But it's all changing. It really is. I can deal with all that, I think. All my siblings changing. But I don't know if I can deal with me.

For now, I have one more amazing senior year left.

Amy

MY BIG SISTER AMY is gone, far away teaching school in South Carolina. And every time someone over twenty-seven or so tries to have a conversation with me, the first thing they always ask is, "So, how is your sister doing?"

Here's the problem. I don't really know.

We don't talk on the phone. I don't especially like talking on the phone. We don't really e-mail, either. We did instant message each other for the first week or so, but then, well, she never got on anymore.

So these people keep asking, "How is your sister doing? Is she enjoying teaching?"

And I go, "Umm . . . I think she is. Uh, I think she's doing pretty good. Last I heard from her she was at least."

"Do you talk to her much?" they ask.

"Well, we instant messaged for a while," I say.

"What's instant messaged?" they ask if they don't know what it is.

And that's the way it goes. Over and over again.

So you can imagine my happiness when, the other day, I was online and realized that Amy was too. I sent her an over-joyed message. She returned one. That was when strange things began to happen.

I wrote her a message. She wrote back saying, "Emily? Are you there?"

I wrote her another message. She wrote back. "Emily? Are you still on?"

Extremely frustrated by now, I wrote a third message.

I heard the telltale "ding" telling me I had an instant message. It was some sort of ugly brown message telling me that my last message could not be sent.

I wrote another frustrated message, banging out something on the keyboard that looked like this: "sdkjfejkl fhkdhfdjhxdjk."

Pretty soon I heard that ding again. "sdkjfejkl fhkdhfdjhxdjk could not be sent."

That's when I gave up. I still don't know how my big sister is doing.

Braving It

I WOKE UP THIS MORNING and didn't feel so hot.

Mom is gone on a trip. Did I mention that?

I didn't feel too good. I didn't feel too horrible, either. But I felt like I was sick, and I knew I had better stay home from school.

I called Dad. He was very unsympathetic and made me cry, but I think that was partially because my emotions were very fragile, due to being sick.

So after that very annoying conversation, I was allowed to stay home. I slept. And slept and slept and slept. When I woke up and went downstairs to eat some fish leftover from last night, the phone rang.

It was my dad, who also happens to be my teacher. He wanted to know if I could come to school for the rest of the day. I agreed, partially because I was feeling a little better but mostly because I felt guilty for staying home. I don't exactly know why. But I felt really icky the whole time I was at school and didn't get much done.

It was so much worse when I got home. Being sick always brings me down. But this takes the cake, what with Dad sending me on guilt trips for the stuff I don't do, no one thinking I'm that sick because I force myself to do so much, and the house falling to pieces before my eyes. The floors are getting dirty, the fridge is starting to smell, and the laundry is piling up. It's horrible.

Ten Random Facts About Me

1. I don't actually mind the smell of skunks.
2. I like cleaning the little gray fuzzies out of hairbrushes. And cleaning the threads and hairs out of vacuum cleaner heads.
3. There are six kids in my family—two older than me, and three younger than me. I love having a big family. I would often just as soon hang out with my family as with friends.
4. One of my favorite foods is pie dough.
5. My favorite character in *The Lord of the Rings* (the movies at least) is Gollum.
6. I'm a Mennonite, which is a denomination of Christianity that shares a lot of principals with the Amish. (But we don't ride around in buggies and we're allowed to use electricity.)
7. I fall asleep more easily in the middle of the day on the living room couch when my siblings are running around than at night in my bed when everything is quiet.

8. I dream every night about pretty much everybody—people I've randomly stood in line with, people whose Xanga sites I've happened across. There's a good chance I've even dreamed about *you* before.

9. I go to a Mennonite school with only 31 other students. Everyone there is really close-knit and friends with everyone else. My dad is even one of my teachers.

10. You know the screensaver that has those pipes that go all over the place and then fade away? Well, sometimes instead of a ball on the end of a pipe joint, there will be a teapot. If a computer is set to the pipes screensaver, I will sit and watch for teapots for hours.

Dreams

I'M THE KIND OF PERSON that if nobody wakes me up, I won't wake up. That's just the long and short of it.

So when I'm sick and staying home from school, and both my mom and big sister happen to be gone, I have to have some system of waking myself up or else I'll sleep until 3:30 PM, when everyone gets home from school.

I came up with a solution. I enlisted the help of my sister's clock radio, which wakes you up with—you guessed it—the radio, instead of annoying beeping that's hard on poor, sick little ears.

This seemed to work other mornings, but this morning, instead of waking up, I started dreaming about *American Idol*.

The girl onstage was amazing. She had gone against all the fashion stylists and everyone who told her what to wear and what to sing. She was wearing a pioneer era dress and was singing a song about wanting to do things that would last for life, not just the here and now. She also kept singing about God. I thought she was amazing. My hero.

But everyone was making fun of her. The next contestant got on stage and sang her own song. The point of this contestant's song was to make fun of the pioneer contestant's song. It was sad. Then Miss Pioneer contestant got back onstage and sang with the other contestant, and they argued about what is important in life while they were singing.

I wanted the pioneer contestant to win so badly. I was so proud of her. But then I realized the third contestant was none other than this awesome guy from my youth group, Brandon!

So while I was sitting there, earnestly trying to decide if I should be rooting for Brandon or this amazing girl who wasn't afraid to voice her beliefs about what is important in life, I woke up and realized that the radio was blaring. Well that explains it.

Blood Draw

I GOT A BLOOD TEST TODAY. Two weeks is a long time to be sick. My mom is beginning to think this isn't just another Emily flu but something else, like mono.

So we drove to the Harrisburg Medical Clinic and went through the whole rigmarole . . . the tight rubber band thing on my upper arm, the spongy ball to squeeze, my mom holding my hand, the doctor telling me I have a good vein, closing my eyes as the needle plunges into my arm.

Wow. Some blood draws don't really hurt. This one did. When it was over, the doctor asked me what I thought of my first blood draw, which was crazy because I've had my blood drawn countless times before. I'm the sick one, you know?

I wonder if I do have something besides Emily flu. I wonder when I'll get better. I'm tired of being sick. I'm falling behind, and I'm feeling useless.

But what can I say? God is with me.

Waiting

I'M STILL SICK.

Yes, it has been almost three weeks now. That is a long time, even for me. It's rather depressing. I got blood drawn a week ago, and Monday they told us they had—gasp!—overlooked my tubes of blood and not sent them in. So I had to get more blood drawn, only the second time it barely hurt at all, thank God. And perhaps sometime soon we shall see if I have some horrible disease or if it's just an extra long bout of Emily flu.

I am having a bit of trouble writing the play, in that it is too short and making it longer is turning out to be harder than expected.

Perhaps tomorrow we will know whether or not I have mono.

When You Are Well

I'M FEELING A LOT BETTER, thank you very much. I thought it would never happen, but look here, it has.

Lots of things have happened recently.

I went to church, and multitudes of people congratulated me on being better now. It was lovely.

In the afternoon, after lunch, I went to Stephy and Justin's house. It was just like old times.

We were messing around with their old video camera when Justin came in and flopped on the bed. I decided to interview him. I said he was a famous poet, since he's always writing poems like "I was walking in the woods, looking for some goods; my feet were bare, then I saw a bear." Stuff like that.

I wanted to name him something else, something besides Justin Smucker, so I scanned the room looking for ideas. My eyes fell on a packet of pictures from Wal-Mart that was sitting on the shelf in the closet.

I pushed the red button. "I am honored to be here, interviewing the renowned poet, Wall Mart," I said.

In a bored monotone Justin replied, "I like walls. Walls inspire me."

Wow, it was funny. I was glad I was behind the camera so it didn't film me laughing. I'm pretty good at laughing silently. But the camera was shaking.

We talked about his past romances with Kay Mart and Dairy Mart, and his current one with Bi Mart.

"Is *Bi* short for something?" I asked.

"There's two of them," said Justin, "you know, cause *bi* means two. Like a bicycle has two wheels."

"So . . . she has two heads?" I asked, not quite understanding.

"No," said Justin, with a perfectly straight face, "there's just two of them."

Stephy and I about died laughing.

Life is so amazing when you are well. The further I get on in my life the more I realize sickness could have the potential to ruin it.

Like with college algebra, for instance. As seniors, Justin and I were going to carpool to the community college and take it together this winter. It would be fun if our friend Bethany would too, but she'd just as soon do the least amount of work required to graduate.

But now, with my recent sickness, my parents aren't sure they want to pay for a college course if I'm gonna get sick in the middle of it and fail. Justin is pretty optimistic. He says I've used up all my sick days this year, so I can't get sick again. I don't think he wants to drive all the way to Albany several times a week by himself.

I think I'll most likely stay well for college algebra. But how can I convince my parents of that?

Communion

SOMETIMES IT FEELS like up is down and red is blue.

And sometimes it feels like I will be sick forever.

Sometimes it feels like I'll never be able to do anything in life, to go anywhere in life, because I'm sick all the time.

And other times it feels like I am missing a huge chunk of life, and in place of that missing chunk is sickness.

Being well was so much fun while it lasted. I thought, *Now, now I can finally make up for lost time. I can hang out with my friends. I can get schoolwork done. I can do things, and* be *somebody.*

Then, communion happened.

It was different this year. Different than it's ever been. I wasn't solemn and serene, humbly thinking about Christ's death. I just wasn't. I was dancing on my way to get the bread. I was happy and jumpy. "I'm well!" I kept thinking, "I'm finally, finally well." And then, something happened that changed everything.

I felt it. The woozy feeling. The funny little headaches springing up the back of my neck. The feelings that *always* precede sickness. I was sitting in church, and I felt them. I didn't know what to do. I wanted to cry; I wanted to cry so badly. But I didn't.

Then the service ended and everyone was so happy for me. So delighted to see me better. Everywhere I went there were people, people, people. They asked me the same question every time. "Are you feeling better?"

And every time I would smile my fake smile, and say the happy words that weren't true. "Yes," I would say. "Yes I am." I wanted them to be true more than anything. But inside I was screaming "No! The woozy feeling! The headaches! I'm getting sick *again*. What is the world coming to?"

Too many people. Too many questions. Too much pain. I went outside. I climbed into the van, away from everyone. And then I cried as I saw my future go up in smoke.

Handing It Over

SOMETHING JUST HAPPENED TO ME. Something greater than I can even fathom.

I am a worrier. I worry about passing tests, about what my parents will say, about not getting things done. I worry so much I make myself sick, and nothing I do seems to make it go away.

Communion night, when I sat in the van and cried, I was confronted with the greatest amount of worries I have ever had in my entire life. Everything I had tried not to think about came pouring over me.

After a year and a half of virtually no sickness, I began to think I would be okay. That if I didn't eat the foods I was allergic to, I would have a normal life. But now? Three bouts of sickness in a row. What does this mean?

What about my schoolwork? Will I be able to get it done if I keep getting sick?

What about my plans? How can I take college algebra if I could get sick at any moment? What happens if I get a job and then fall sick for two weeks?

And my future? What about my future? Any option I can think of—getting a job, going to college, doing voluntary service, attending a Bible institute, even becoming a wife and mother—would never work. How could it, if I could fall sick at any given moment and be out for two weeks at a time?

It isn't like this is so far off in the future, you know. This is my senior year. I'll graduate, hopefully. I'll turn eighteen whether I like it or not.

I was worried sick. That was all I could think about. All night. All day. Worry, worry, worry. There was nothing I could do to make it go away.

"I can't handle this!" I told God one night. "This is too much for me. *You* were the one who allowed me to get sick, *you* take them."

I pried my worries out of my mind like old gum from the inside of a trash can. I told God what the worries were and why I had them.

Then I handed them over. "Here God, these are your worries now. Not mine."

And they were gone. Bing bang boom. Just like that.

I thought about school, about college, about a job . . . everything that had caused me to worry before. And I smiled to myself. Someone else was taking care of it for me.

I cannot describe how that felt. Like a cool breeze on a hot day. Like stepping out from a hideously ugly room into an unbelievably beautiful garden. Only a million times better.

Walls

I DECIDED I WOULD do something cool and spin around with my eyes closed, count to twenty-one, and write about whatever I was pointing to. So I did, and guess what? I was pointing at the wall.

Now, there are a limited number of things you can say about a wall. I could say that walls inspire me and make the people who get that inside joke laugh, only it would be a lie because walls don't inspire me. Not really.

A blank wall might inspire me to paint a dragon on it or doodle on it while I'm supposed to be doing my homework, but this particular wall isn't even a nice white inspiring wall. It's painted in a funny print of baby blue and tan.

Amy and Jenny's room also has some random splotches

of paint on it. When Jenny was three, she and I shared that room, while Amy had the room I have now. Ah Jenny . . . she ate all my gum, scribbled in all my books, and decorated the walls with any paint she could get her hands on.

But she didn't paint this room. Mom did, all blue and tan with a Peter Rabbit border. I ripped the border down when I got the room, but the blue and tan stayed.

I don't like tan.

There is one interesting thing about these walls. A certain splotch of baby blue paint looks like a mermaid.

That is all.

Analogies

I LOVE COMING UP with analogies. I made up one about my current state of sickness last night.

Imagine you were slowly sinking in a bog. You would have three choices in how you would react:

1. Panic
2. Struggle, hoping against hope that someone will pull you out
3. Resign yourself to the situation

Being sick is kind of like that. At least, being sick for this long without really knowing why, that is.

But what scares me is that I'm not panicking or struggling or hoping against hope that someone, or something, will pull me out of this situation. Slowly, I'm resigning myself to it. I don't know why. I don't really want to be resigned to it, but I can't seem to help it. Plus, the other options don't look too inviting either. I've been struggling, but it wears a person out until they get tired of it. And panicking just makes me feel worse.

It's like my life is on "pause" right now. I don't know what's going to happen to me. I don't know if I have some horrid disease, or if something in this house or Oregon itself is making me sick, and thus, I would have to move.

So here I am, sick, waiting for something to happen.

I don't really want to go back to school right now. I know that is horrible, since I'm so behind and need to get caught up. But that's just it. School for me right now represents a big pile of "behind." Like I'm on the bottom of the down escalator, trying to get to the top. Yeah, I know, another analogy. Analogies are amazing.

Did I tell you that all my test results came back negative? I have no idea where this sickness is heading. None at all.

More Plans

TODAY I FINISHED writing the church play. Finished it for good, hopefully. It's about all these unique characters who are jealous of each other. We're planning to perform it around Thanksgiving. Did I mention that? So the characters learn to be thankful for what they have, instead of being jealous of everyone else. Because someone is jealous of them.

Tomorrow the preachers and their wives are going to anoint me with oil and pray for me as instructed in James 5:14–15.

I was hoping that today I would get better. That's just what I had in my mind. However, I actually felt worse than ever.

I still don't know where I'm going. But I do know this. I'm going to fight like a mad catfish to do the play. I must do it. I have to do it. I am going to do it unless for some reason God doesn't want me to.

So here's my plan: when they anoint me with oil, I'll get better. Doesn't the Bible say that the prayer of the faithful shall save the sick? Something like that.

I don't think I'll get sick again for a while. I'm going to work really hard on my schoolwork and try to get it done early because I often get sick in the spring.

I probably won't be able to get a job, but I really want to

do college algebra. I think I could get by if I got sick for a few days because Justin could fill me in on what I missed. And I *will* do the play. I have to.

No Show

THERE IS A POINT when something amazing is about to happen to you that a tremendous fear rises—a fear that something will go wrong, and you won't have your amazing something after all. So you desperately, *desperately* try to correct the kinks and make it happen, and then you fall flat on your face.

I counted on that play. It was going to be my breakthrough. I had it all figured out. Why does everything go wrong when I have it all figured out?

I finished the play. I thought, *What now?* So, I wrote a desperate, long letter to Jeanette, our youth sponsor, asking questions about different aspects of the play, wanting to make sure it was going to happen.

I didn't want it to sound desperate, but I was scared as I wrote it . . . horribly scared. There was always another question, another thing that could go wrong, and I was fervently trying to keep down the "What if I don't get better?" questions that kept popping up inside my head. I wanted her to answer right away with an answer to everything.

She didn't.

It didn't take me long to realize it wasn't the questions I had written down, but the question I hadn't. *If I don't get better, who's going to take the play and run with it?*

The answer to that question is no one. There is no guarantee I will get better and stay better.

I talked to Jeanette about it, and we came to the conclusion that I just can't do it with the way my health has been. The play, *my* play, is off.

The Wish

I HAVE A FUNNY WISH right now that a digital camcorder will mysteriously come in the mail for me. I want a digital camcorder so bad. Every day I check the front porch to see if one has arrived.

I don't dream about being better anymore. Even being better means I could get sick again—falling behind, and failing, and losing all, and clawing my way to the top only to get sick again and plummet to the ground.

And somehow, even getting a digital camcorder from some unknown benefactress seems more likely than getting well does.

The Magic Potion

PEOPLE GIVE ME GIFTS. Cards, mostly. The loveliest one was from all the students at school. Stephy wrote a poem.

Bethany is very loyal. She visited me once last week and brought me a gift from her mother. It was a wonderful gift basket, with crackers and easy cheese (you know, that cheese you can squirt out of a bottle), two white shirts, and amazing markers to use on the shirts, so I can design my own.

Then, Sunday, she came again, bringing a present from herself. This one contained a glass slipper bottle filled with bubble bath, a green fuzzy scarf, and some American Girl lotion.

Phebe had wondered if she could come see me and bring some other girls along. I thought it would be wonderful.

A knock sounded on the door. Was it them? When the door opened, a long line of beautiful young ladies poured in, bearing a gigantic box covered with gold paper. In an attempt to cheer me up, they had filled the box with every wonderful and delightful thing imaginable (except for a digital camcorder). There were clothes and hot pink shoes and tea and a goblet and cards that said the nicest things. There were mountains (okay, small hills) of candy, which was a little unfortunate since Mom had been after me to cut back on sweets to boost my immune system. There were beautiful, inspiring, lovely notebooks. There was a very interesting movie and a very interesting book. But deep in that golden box was the most wonderful thing of all. The thing I've been longing for ever since this sickness started. A bottle of magic potion.

It looked suspiciously like a bottle of Kiwi Strawberry Snapple, one of the few fruit drinks I could actually drink. But the gold label clearly read "Magic Potion."

I didn't want to drink it all at once. I wanted to savor it. So I took a little sip right then, and saved the rest for later.

Every time I thought about it, I took another sip from the wonderful bottle of magic potion. But perhaps I savored it too much. Or perhaps the potion should have had a gold label on it that read "refrigerate after opening." Or perhaps I'm just stupid. In any case, the bottle of magic potion was *not* refrigerated after opening.

I didn't even think about it until tonight, days later, when I again pawed through the gold box of gifts. I was actually looking for a candy fix, but I came across the magic potion. It wasn't quite half-empty yet.

Was it bad? I took a small taste. It tasted a little funny, but not too bad. I decided I had better drink it now, before it got worse.

I took a big swig.

I felt something solid and furry in my mouth.

I spit the big swig back into the bottle.

Then, I sadly poured it down the drain. Such was the fate of my magic potion.

Singing Penguins

HOW LONG HAS IT BEEN? I am still sick. If it were not so, I would have told you.

I am still sick. What more is there to say?

I am still living.

I am still dreaming. Lovely, wonderful dreams. Where would I be if it weren't for my dreams?

As far as how my life is going for real, it is considerably less exciting than my dreams. No singing penguins, no four-teen-year-old friends deciding to get married and live in a yellow and black backpack, no dying from a snakebite while my dad shops around trying to find the cheapest hospital deal.

So my life is slowly plodding along. I'm drinking bottled water and eating pills that are supposed to make me well and waiting for lab tests to come back and reading a book about dragons and arguing with my little sister.

We were having an argument today, and this is how it ended:

Me: That doesn't make sense.

Jenny: Well what you said made sense to me but I want to pretend it didn't. So there.

Hobbit Poetry

ONCE WHEN I READ *The Hobbit*, I tried to understand it better by writing down all the poems in my ladybug notebook. I had always skipped the poetry or skimmed through it to get on with the story. But this time I really wanted to absorb it.

Needless to say, after the first three poems, I stumbled upon a long one and gave up. But that is not the point of this story.

One poem was a funny one about breaking Bilbo Baggins' plates and bending his forks. One was a fascinating one that was so much fun to recite, all about "Far over the misty mountains cold/ To dungeons deep and caverns old." I don't even remember the third one, except for the first line, which replays over and over in my head.

"O! What are you doing/And where are you going?" it asks.

I don't know. Seriously, where *am* I going? Nowhere. I should be going somewhere. Sure I'm sick, but I have to be heading down some path. What path am I heading down? Huh? Huh?

And what am I doing? What am I doing at all? I am lying around all day feeling miserable. I'm asking myself where I'm going and what I'm doing. I am lazy and I hate it. But there doesn't seem to be another way.

The Seven Princesses

I'VE BEEN WRITING MORE. Usually when I'm sick I don't write much, since I don't get inspired. But today was different.

I saw a list of the books my sister wants to get someday, and one of them was *The Ordinary Princess*. At least I think that's what the list said. In any case, it reminded me of a book I once read called *The Ordinary Princess,* which was good except for one thing. On the cover, if you looked closely at the ordinary princess's left foot, you could see her toenails were red. So all throughout the book I was waiting for her to paint her toenails red. But she never did.

This inspired me to write a story about a princess who painted her toenails red. However, once I began writing, it quickly turned into a story of seven princesses—Adaline, Brumhilda, Carmelinda, Delphinium, Esmerilda, Fanica, and Grum-ah-lum-ah-tum-tum—who keep drinking forbidden potions that make them do crazy stuff. I probably will never finish the story, but it was fun to write.

I think I'll end up writing for children. I've never really wanted to do anything else. Indeed, I've never really wanted to *read* anything else. Children's books do something for me that other books cannot. They take me places when I want to escape.

Part Positive

ONE BLOOD TEST CAME out part positive. It was the blood test for West Nile fever. Apparently, according to the test, I might have West Nile and I might not. To know for sure, I need to have further, extremely expensive testing.

Wait, how does that work? I might have it and I might not? What kind of idiotic test result is that? I never knew test results *could* be like that.

My mom is all up in the air because West Nile has no cure. I'm more inclined to think I don't even have West Nile. I mean, I get sick all the time and there's never a name for it. It's just another bout of Emily flu. So I have a theory that I'm allergic to something in Oregon or maybe something in this house, and that's what's making me sick.

When I was twelve, my mom took me to a doctor in Creswell who did lots of allergy testing. I restricted my diet, and it helped a lot with my constant sicknesses. So now Mom and Dad are thinking, *Well, Dr. Hanson helped us so much back then, I wonder if he can help us again now?*

I normally feel very uncomfortable around doctors, specifically male doctors, and don't particularly like visiting them. But I am really looking forward to going to see Dr. Hanson. I want him to say, "You are allergic to Oregon. Go move in with relatives." And then I could go live in South Carolina with Amy or something.

I've always been jealous of girls in books who get to move to a totally new place, but those girls in books never *wanted* to move. I still read books like that and think, *Are you crazy? Why are you so upset about leaving your family and living with your cool aunt and uncle at a super duper cool school in Switzerland?*

Don't get me wrong. I love my family. I love my friends. I love my church. But what I want most is adventure and wellness, and the idea of getting both in one fell swoop by moving somewhere else is my greatest desire right now.

That's why I'm looking forward to seeing Dr. Hanson. If he said "Move," my parents would listen to him.

Insomnia

I ALWAYS THOUGHT staying up all night was stupid. People talk about how much fun it is, staying up all night with your buddies and acting crazy, but I never saw the appeal. I mean seriously. There are lots of other crazy and fun things to do with your buddies that don't require turn-ing yourself into an annoying grump the next day. And you need to get your sleep sometime, so why not at night, where sleep belongs? Sure, I've had insomnia before. And I do like staying up late, especially at sleepovers, but not all night.

Well look at me now. I just stayed up all night.

It's not like I wanted to stay up all night. I didn't even have buddies to hang out with (unless you count my little sis who got up in the middle of the night to use the bathroom). I just . . . did it. Accidentally.

So now, here I am. 7:57 AM. I have a splitting headache and am as wide awake as a fish.

Stupid insomnia.

The good news is that now I can say I accidentally stayed up all night, which sounds kinda cool.

Random fact: nearly every night, sometime between 11:00 PM and 4:00 AM, my brother Steven bangs on the wall in his sleep.

West Nile

HERE'S THE THING ABOUT high hopes: When you're brought back down to reality, it is such a shocking experi-ence that you cry. You can't help it.

I can't at least.

Yes, I cried coming out of Dr. Hanson's office. Yes I was embarrassed. Yes I wished I could stop. But I couldn't, because Dr. Hanson said none of the things I wanted him to say.

What he said was, "According to the test results and her symptoms, and judging from what I've seen in other people, I think she has West Nile."

Um, hello? The *specialist* thinks I *don't* have West Nile. What about that? Huh? Huh?

When that was brought up, Dr. Hanson said there is a chance the specialist had ulterior motives in saying I didn't have West Nile. Good grief. Why would he have ulterior motives? But of course Mom believes Dr. Hanson over mysterious specialist guy.

Dr. Hanson says I should take fever baths to try and get West Nile out of my system. Basically, he says, when you are sick your body temperature increases to fight the disease. So if I take a long hot bath and force myself to stay mostly submerged, my temperature will rise and help get West Nile out of my system. That is assuming, of course, that I even have West Nile.

Honestly, the idea of taking a long, hot bath didn't seem exceedingly daunting until I took my first bath tonight.

How can I explain the horror of it? Of being submerged in hot water, all but my face, which had sweat pouring off it? It doesn't sound horrible. It really doesn't. But when I think of it, and how weak I was afterward, and having to do it six more times, I think that maybe if I can get through it I'll be able to handle being tortured for my faith someday or something.

Maybe if I do all seven fever baths, and nothing positive happens healthwise, I'll be able to convince my parents that I don't have West Nile, and we need to keep searching.

Practical Jokes

HOW IS MY LIFE GOING? Well, for one thing, I've started entertaining myself by commenting on my mom's blog under a different name. It's so funny, because no matter how often I do it, she never realizes it's me.

Mom: Did you see this comment on my site? Isn't it so sweet? [Looks lovingly at the comment.]

Me: Do you know who Julia Adams is? [Trying hard not to laugh.]

Mom: No, do you?

I burst out laughing.

Realization dawns on Mom's face. She looks startled, then surprised, then she too is shrieking with laughter. "I thought it was some sweet, prim, little, conservative girl from Iowa!" she gasps.

In other news, right now the upstairs hall resembles an obstacle course. And yet, no one thinks to move anything.

One more thing. A recent trip to the doctor revealed that perhaps I should not eat so much sugar. So now my tea is sweetened with honey (which isn't as bad as I thought it would be) and cookies are getting replaced with crackers.

Without Me

I AM NOT GOING TO be in the school Christmas skit. All the casting was done without me. It didn't surprise me, but it still hurt. Like no one even thinks I'm gonna get better anymore.

I think all this is getting to me, all this acting I should be doing but am not. Seriously. Like the dream I had last night.

In my dream, I went back to school. I thought I was better, but I sort of wasn't. And so things went along in odd ways and I tried to push away the bits of lingering sickness.

And then, Harmony Headings asked me to be in a skit that she and some other girls were doing for the Christmas program. I was delighted. Since I couldn't be in the normal play, at least I could be in this one.

I was hoping so badly that I could be the main character, which was a girl. Harmony cast the parts, one by one. She didn't cast anyone to be the girl. I knew it would be me. I was so excited! But she didn't say it was me. She just didn't say anything.

"So what am I, the understudy?" I said, joking.

"Yes," she said.

I was heartbroken, aghast, scandalized. I couldn't believe it. "What?"

I ran out of there, trying not to cry. I woke up from the dream sad. I really, really want to get better. To act. I just want life to stop moving along without me.

Work Craze

I AM ON A WORK CRAZE. I want to make $100 in three days. So I slave away doing odd chores and Mom pays me.

Why am I so desperate for money, you may ask?

A digital camcorder. That's what I want. A digital camcorder that actually has decent sound and picture quality. I want it so much. So now, instead of wishing for one to show up at my door, I am working, even though I feel icky. I wash down furniture and organize books. I sweep floors and do dishes. But vacuuming floors is too hard.

Despite that, Mom is convinced I'm getting better. Dad is too, but somehow Dad always seems to think I'm getting better. It drives me nuts. I am *not* getting better. The fever baths did nothing for me, except make me realize that if I can survive them I can survive doing a couple hours of work each day, as long as I have visions of digital camcorders looming in my head.

However, Mom is so confident I'm getting better she is insisting I go to the Smucker gathering at the coast in four days. Fine. I love hanging out with my Smucker relatives, but I don't love doing it sick.

I suppose, though, if I can survive the fever baths I can survive this.

Smucker Gathering

MY TRIP TO THE COAST started off boring and uneventful enough. There were hardly any people there, and Rosie and Phil, who were supposed to tell us which rooms we were in, were out walking on the beach.

I ended up in a dumb room with uncomfortable bunk beds and no door. Mom and I tacked a blanket over the doorway, but it still didn't offer much as far as privacy goes. Especially since it was kind of in the middle of everything.

I am sorry to say that for most of the weekend, I wandered around not sure what to do. Everybody always seemed to be doing *something* that I was too sick to participate in. Walking on the beach or playing ping-pong required energy, and card games required brain power, both of which I lacked.

I had horrific insomnia that first night, partially because of my uncomfortable bed and partially because I usually have insomnia. Sometimes I zoned out, and later I couldn't decide if I had been sleeping or not. It's hard to tell sometimes when you don't dream.

I heard a rustle. It was some cousins and uncles getting up to go fishing. I thought maybe I would get up and talk to them, since I had nothing better to do.

Well, did I have a time getting out of that stupid bed. It was tucked in so tight, and the bed above me was so low that I was pretty much stuck. That gave me claustrophobia. Yikes. I began to get hot. And desperate. *Calm down, Emily. Think. Move yourself this way, then that way.*

With only a few muscles pulled, I was free of the evil bed. Whew.

After chatting with the fishermen a bit, I stayed awake until other people began to get up, and then crawled into my parents' bed. It was actually comfortable. Somehow, despite that, I still had trouble getting to sleep. But I finally did.

My one beautiful memory of the trip was that evening, when Stephy and I were sitting on a futon talking. Most of the others were watching the movie *End of the Spear*. I could see the left half of the screen, but a pillar blocked my view of the right half. So I started jokingly trying to figure out what was going on by describing to Stephy what I could see.

Stephy, who due to the same pillar could only see the right half of the screen, giggled and described what she could see. Whenever the natives spoke their language, I would read half the English subtitles and she would read the other half. We could have moved, of course. But it was so crazy and fun, exactly what hanging out with cousins should be.

We decided to sleep on that futon that night. The living room had been reserved for the guys, but there were way more futons down there than they needed, while upstairs, where the girls were, bedding was so scarce that Stephy needed to sleep on the floor. Plus, there was a huge lack of privacy anyway. My room wasn't the only one without a door.

I slept so much better that night. We whispered all kinds of secrets and in the morning, when we left, I thought maybe the trip wasn't a total waste after all.

The Vacuum Cleaner

THE SCISSORS SAT on top of my desk in a goblet. The intercom lay on the floor. Only one thing stood between me and them: the vacuum cleaner that was hanging from my hair.

If I reached into the drawer behind me, could I reach the dagger I had gotten in Kenya? I doubted it, and even if I could, the thing wasn't very sharp.

I looked at the intercom again. Could I reach it? I shifted the vacuum cleaner as much as I could in that tiny room, turned my head away so my hair wouldn't get pulled, and reached blindly in that direction. My hand connected with a button of some sort. Hoping it was the right one, I pushed. "Can someone please come help me?" I called.

Steven, who was downstairs doing his homework, heard my desperate cry and came to rescue me. He opened the door and burst out laughing.

"What happened?" he asked.

Sheepishly, I explained my unusual predicament. My room hasn't been vacuumed in a while, so I was trying to do a thorough job. I was sucking ancient dust bunnies out from under the bookshelf with the hose, when I felt a sharp pain in my head. I hadn't thought about the fact that the head of the vacuum cleaner is still sucking, even if you're using the hose. I also hadn't thought about the fact that long, loose hair is never safe around the head of a vacuum cleaner. And thus, the machine managed to grab my hair and wind it tightly around the beater bar.

But it all ended well. Steven fetched the scissors, and I'm not bald.

The Christmas Program

I KEEP HAVING TO go places I don't want to go. One of the big reasons is this thing called the Christmas Program.

I looked at the script for the program once, and it nearly broke my heart. My name wasn't on it, not anywhere. I guess

I already knew I wasn't in it, but just seeing those names—Bethany, Justin, Stephy, but no Emily . . . I don't know. It felt like an extra punch in the stomach.

My dad wanted to go over the script with me and have me tell him what needed to be done. Where should the characters stand as they say their lines? When should they enter and exit? I explained it all to him.

My dad also wanted me to help him direct it. But he had an odd way of getting the kids to practice, with no real acting until right at the end. I went to school twice to "help direct," but I really didn't do much.

I went to the big program on Wednesday even though I felt horrible. I didn't want to go, but I did because I realized it was my duty. That's what pushed me out the door.

As soon as we got there, Matt and I rushed upstairs to the balcony. I really did not want to have to talk to anyone.

I watched the play and felt so removed. I couldn't help but think about all the "what ifs." *What if it was me on that stage performing? What if I had actually directed this thing? Think of how wonderful it would be!* I was imagining myself on that bench, waiting for my turn to perform and whispering to my neighbor. Imagining myself onstage and hearing the audience laughing at the funny thing I said. Imagining myself standing on those risers, singing my heart out. It was exactly where I should have been. Where it was normal to be.

I sort of felt like I didn't exist.

At the end of the program, Dad got up and gave a little speech thanking anyone who had helped out in even the tiniest of ways. I had a fleeting hope he would mention me, and I could exist for a little bit after all, but he didn't. I started to tear up. I was barely able to keep from crying, I felt so horrible.

For the rest of the evening, I couldn't think about it or else I would almost cry, and it would take all my effort plus remembering my friend Alfonso trying to do a cartwheel on Rollerblades to thwart it. If you have ever seen someone try to do a cartwheel on Rollerblades, you will understand why it is a funny enough memory to stop tears.

After the program, my friends brought me food and hung out with me, which was wonderful. But I left fairly soon after that.

Coincidences

ONCE, WHEN I WAS YOUNGER, I was eating clam chowder when I saw a funny clam that was black and bluish. I ate it anyway.

Later, I drank some lemonade, and it hurt my throat.

After that, whenever I drank lemonade and it hurt my throat, I thought it was because I had eaten a weird black and bluish clam and it had somehow damaged my throat.

It's odd, sometimes, how when two things happen at the

same time it feels like one caused the other, when in reality it was a total coincidence.

The worst, I think, is when I walk into the room and everybody bursts out laughing. It always takes me a bit to realize that no one is laughing at me; indeed, they probably didn't even see me. They just happened to be laughing at some random joke when I walked in.

A Magical Realization

EVERY YEAR, my dad takes us to a football game because he's just so nice, but I've only gone twice. I'm not terribly big on sports. The first year I got a subscription to *American Girl* magazine instead and last year I got a gigantic book. This year, Dad took me to see the play *A Christmas Carol*.

It was a good play. It made me happy inside. We walked back to the car, and the lights of the city, and the crisp, cold air, and being with my dad, who took me to see the play even though he doesn't even really like plays . . . it was all so magical.

We went to Safeway, then, because Dad had to get groceries. Right in front of the door was a display of roses. I said, "Dad, do you ever get Mom roses for no reason?"

"Well, sometimes," he said. "Would you like it if I got you roses for no reason?"

He was seriously offering to buy me a dozen roses!

There, way in the back, were a dozen beautiful, perfect, multicolored roses. And then, as I was standing beside my dad and looking at my beautiful roses, I was struck by a perfect thought.

You see, my family is planning to visit Kenya this spring, and after that, those who had saved enough money were going to take a detour to Yemen before coming home. But oops, my cousin Keith got engaged, and his wedding was scheduled over the time we were planning to be in Yemen. So that part of the trip was canceled, and I, who had been desperately saving my pennies, was very disappointed.

But right then, at that magical moment, standing beside my dad in Safeway and looking at my roses, it struck me. With my Yemen money I'd have enough to buy my digital camcorder, plus extra, for Christmas presents.

I felt like the happiest girl in the world.

It was wonderful.

Randomness

I LOVE MY WATCH. In a book I just read, the characters smashed their watches with hammers, because they were so sick of clocks running their lives. It was cool in the book, but when I looked at my watch, I knew I could never smash it because I love it so much.

I don't know why I keep pens I don't like. I probably keep them because, no matter how many cool pens I get, there is always the chance all my cool pens will end up at school and on my bed and in my purses and in my mom's pen cup. It's happened before. And running out of pens is horrid. Worse than running out of paper, because you can always write on your skin or a napkin or your clothes if all else fails.

I once got a cheap backpack that lasted practically forever, and I loved it more than any backpack I've ever had before or since. I love things like that.

Snail mail is so much more fun to receive than e-mail, but I don't send out snail mail. I would love to be the sort of person who always remembers to write letters to people, but I'm not.

I love reading about characters who are unlike any characters I've ever read about before.

I got a new alarm clock today. My old one has a crack in it, and the second hand fell off and is lying at the bottom of the clock. I used to read in bed with it by holding down on the snooze button, but then the battery would run down, my alarm would go off late, and I wouldn't get up early enough to finish my homework. Maybe I should smash my old alarm clock with a hammer.

Sometimes I wish silver didn't tarnish.

There is a book under my mattress about how God is like

an apple. You know, like God the Father, God the Son, and God the Holy Spirit are like the core, skin, and flesh of an apple. But I don't think God is like an apple. I think God is sort of like light. Because light is very hard to understand, if you really think about it. How it somehow contains every color we've ever seen, and yet we can't actually see the colors unless something breaks them apart. There are a lot of things about light I can't understand, and I think God is like that. You just can't understand how he is three in one, because your understanding is limited.

I wonder why everyone loves to give out little wallet-sized pictures of themselves. I have done that twice in my life. I did it because it was the cool thing to do, and then later I thought, *Ugh! I'm doing something I don't like to do, and the only reason I'm doing it is to be just like everyone else!* I immediately stopped. I'm not trying to make fun of people who give out wallet-sized pictures of themselves smiling, by the way. I just wonder why everyone does it. Does everyone else love to have smiling faces of their friends around them all the time, or does everyone just do it because it's the cool thing to do?

The Notice

MY FRIEND Justin Doutrich (who I normally refer to as J. D.) recently posted this on his blog:

NOTICE:

If you are a young lady near the age of twenty-years old, one Justin Doutrich has need of your services. The esteemed company, Swartzendruber Construction, is having a Christmas supper, and each attendant is required to bring an attractive date. This is a one-time offer with no strings attached, no long-term relationships hidden in the fine print, truly a free meal for having to put up with the above-mentioned male figure for an entire evening (6:00 PM–10:00 PM). Resumes are not required but e-mails are accepted (use link on this site). Requirements include: the applicant must be alive, at least moderately attractive, have a nice demeanor, and smell pleasant. Submit all applications during normal working hours.

Your country needs you.

I thought it was funny, but of course I didn't apply, being only seventeen and quite sick. But apparently poor J. D. had trouble getting a date, despite his advertisement of sorts (there is a lack of eligible females in our church), because Dad came into my room the other night and said, "Just so you know, J. D. is probably going to call you soon and ask you to his Christmas supper."

I smiled. "So he called you up and asked your permission, huh?"

"Yeah," Dad said. "He wondered if it was okay to take you, since you're only seventeen. But I don't think it counts as a real date."

Because, after all, it is sort of a Mennonite tradition to not date for real until you are eighteen.

I thought it would be fun. I thought I could probably go, even though I was sick. But I also began to think maybe I never wanted to go on a date for real, because despite there being nothing romantic whatsoever about our date, I felt nervous and awkward about everything.

I was nervous waiting for my phone to ring. I was nervous talking to him, which is odd, because I've known J. D. forever. He is my brother's best friend. Talking to him should not be weird.

I was also nervous about what to wear. Was it formal or informal? I decided on a white turtleneck sweater, which was the perfect choice, up until the moment I actually had to wear it.

I was hot and flustered, nervous and scatterbrained, sick and weak. He would be here any minute, and I still needed this, and that, and this other thing . . .

I heard a knock on the door. Oh no! Was he here already? I hurriedly filled my purse, borrowed from Mom, as out of the corner of my eye I saw someone let J. D. in and offer him a seat.

"Emily!" I heard Mom say softly, in her why-on-earth-did-you-do-*that* voice.

Huh? What had I done? I looked up.

Oh duh. I should have been the one opening the door and offering him a seat. I should have at least *looked* at him. What was wrong with me?

Thankfully, it was better once we got on our way, and much, *much* better once we got there.

There were two tables pushed together. J. D.'s boss Ben and his wife Ruth, my cousin Jessi and her husband Kevin, and another couple I didn't know sat at one table, while J. D., Brandon, Phebe, and I sat at the other table.

We had so much fun, us four. We made jokes the whole time, mostly centered around the disgusting orange soup we were served. It was awesome hanging out with them, because, being so sick, I don't get to hang out with my friends that often.

Somehow things were less awkward going back home, and we had interesting conversations about writing and fantasy. And then I was home, and everybody wanted to know how everything had gone.

Despite the initial nervousness, it was such a lovely evening. Just getting picked up at my house, and having my chair pulled out for me, and eating fancy food (and gross orange soup)—the whole thing made me feel so special.

I am happy inside.

Daphne

MY DIGITAL CAMCORDER came in the mail today! Unfortunately I can't film anything yet, because I need to buy tape. But it makes me indescribably happy just to take it out of the box and look at it. It is so lovely.

I named it Daphne.

Still Sick

WELL, WELL, WELL. Christmas has passed, and I am still sick. I always had it in my mind that I would be better by Christmas. Mom did too. Maybe we all did.

But we were wrong.

So now what? Am I going to be sick forever?

On a lighter note, I have decided to become a princess. Don't think I'm crazy. I'm just trying to cope here. If I wanna be a princess, who's gonna stop me?

Amy gave me a very wonderful pair of princess shoes for Christmas.

Yesterday, I got a call from Louise, an older lady from our

church. She asked me what color I preferred in dresses: sage green or dusty plumb. I said sage green, since I have been obsessed with green of late. And then she and three other ladies from church brought it over. A sage green wonder. A dress. The sort of dress a princess would wear to dinner.

Resolutions

ISN'T IT ODD HOW THE TINIEST, most insignificant things can do the most damage?

Perhaps if I had put on mosquito repellent or decided not to go outside. Maybe if I had swatted it or worn long sleeves instead of short ones, I could be going to school tomorrow, to study some hard, yet surprisingly interesting physics. Then I might head off to community college to take a class of college algebra. Imagine being able to comprehend those complicated math problems.

It's been four months since I got sick. Since then, I've been well for three weeks, near the beginning, but it probably wasn't true wellness. More like an illusion that I was well, though the West Nile was still there, dormant, waiting to attack again. Assuming, of course, that West Nile is what I actually have.

Part of me thought I'd be well by Christmas. The other part of me thought I would never ever get better. I pushed everything up to that deadline. *If I can get well by Christmas,* I told myself, *I'll be able to graduate this year without too much of a problem.* That was the main goal.

But look here. Christmas is gone. School is starting tomorrow. And I'm not going.

I used to have my life planned out. If you asked me, "Are you going to college?" I would say, "Next year I'll probably take a few courses at community college. Especially writing courses."

If you asked me, "Are you going to Bible school?" I would say, "I'll probably go to Biblical Mennonite Alliance (BMA) Bible Institute next year."

And most of all, if you asked me, "Are you going to graduate this year?" I would say, "Yes."

I suppose they weren't definite plans. But they were plans, and now I have no plans. Because now if you ask me, "Are you going to college?" I will say, "Maybe, but I'm afraid I could get sick in the middle of classes, and then where would I be?" or "Maybe, if the effects of West Nile have worn off by then."

Because mostly I don't think anymore. I don't plan. I just exist.

I wonder what my New Year's resolutions would have been if I had never been bitten by that infected mosquito. Would I have resolved to move mountains? To conquer the world?

Because now, all I find myself resolving is to do the two

things I would have taken for granted. To get well and to graduate. But what's the point of resolving to do those things? It's not like I can help it if my West Nile decides to stay. What can I do if I open a textbook and find I can't even comprehend what it says anymore? And that is why it's so frustrating. I'm a puppet on a string, totally out of control of my own destiny.

The world would be an easier place if everyone I knew had gotten West Nile in their past, that way I wouldn't have to spend so much time explaining to people what it was like. So maybe someday someone else will have the same thing, and I'll make their life a little easier, because I'll know how to empathize.

Or maybe I'll become a missionary in some exotic place, and I'll get tortured for my faith, but I'll know I'll be able to make it, because I made it through this.

Or maybe I'm just supposed to learn not to worry about my future.

I don't know.

John McCane

SOMETIMES IT SEEMS LIKE I get weaker and weaker every day. First, milk jugs got heavier. Then I started walking slower and slower, and leaning on furniture more and more. They joked about me needing a cane, or a walker, or a wheelchair, and then Mom considered buying me one. A cane, that is.

Yesterday, she actually did it. I now have a cane. And of course it seems crazy for a seventeen-year-old to have a cane, but it's so nice to have it to lean on.

It was boring when I got it—a black, metal cane with a plastic handle. I glued a pink ribbon on it and tied it in a bow. I added fairytale stickers: a princess, a prince, a gnome, and a magical bird.

I named my cane John McCane.

I am wondering what will people say? What will they think? To see me, Emily Smucker, with a cane?

Maybe when I go places I can discreetly, you know, lean on furniture or something, and leave John McCane behind.

Maybe I need him too much to do that.

We shall see.

Back to School

I HAVE TREMENDOUS amounts of trouble doing my schoolwork, and I'm not sure why. I like to blame it on my sickness, but I have a secret fear it's not that complicated and I'm just lazy.

Sometimes, it feels like sickness makes it harder to think, and other times I think just fine. Sometimes I think sickness makes me lazier, and sometimes I think that's a really lame excuse.

It's usually easier to just push it from my mind and think about something else. But right now, school and schoolwork have been on my mind quite a bit, because I went yesterday. I went to school, really and truly.

Not that I wanted to. But I basically had to, because Dad is anxious to start on our senior Bible class. I need that class to graduate. I can't take it by myself later, because a big chunk of the class is discussing things. So now, once a week for half a day I have to go to school.

Anyway, I went to school yesterday, cane and all. I was so proud of myself.

But it wore me out.

And I hated school.

I should have loved school. I loved school last year. The whole student body was like one giant clique, and I was the center of it. I mean, not the *exact* center, but everybody was my friend, and I knew all the jokes and the inside stories and the latest things people had done. And yes, everyone is still my friend now, but I don't fit in anymore.

At first I thought, *Everything is the same. Why don't I fit in?* Then I realized that I've changed. Or maybe just my outlook on life has changed.

Me and them, we have totally different lives now.

More Randomness

IF I HAD ONE WISH, I don't know what I'd wish for.

Had to go to school today. It was noisy. Gave me a headache. Then some kid was scared to sit by me because he thought he could get West Nile. Hello, would I be going to school if I was contagious, potentially ruining everyone else's life? I don't think so.

All right, I'm grumpy. I'll admit it. I wasn't trying to make fun of the kid in the above-mentioned paragraph.

Violets are purple.

Ever since we got home from school, my little sister has been begging me to play Phase 10, our favorite family game, with her. I guess I accidentally promised to yesterday. *Arg zarg.*

A lot of people spell *a lot* as *alot* like it is one word and for some reason it annoys me terribly.

Someday I'll do something more exciting than going to school half the day and watching some kid try to play a board game and work on yearbook at the same time. I can't wait.

Once a girl took a picture of me for the yearbook. Or maybe she took two. Anyway, I think that's the first picture of me for the yearbook, except for the picture of the whole school. I was also making some pretty interesting faces, because it would take her too long to fiddle with the camera and I would get impatient and make an odd face.

Recently, I ate some lima beans. Actually it was before Christmas, but it feels like recently. I always thought I liked lima beans, but I guess I don't after all.

Especially since I once named a cat Lima Bean. Why would you name a cat after something you don't like?

The lima bean is also called a butter bean. Isn't that weird? Why would you call a bean a butter bean? Either it's butter or it's a bean.

However, I normally wouldn't care if someone called a lima bean a butter bean. I'm not always this grumpy.

Reading is fun. I have never understood how someone could not like to read. It's one of the great mysteries of life, way up there with why so many people love coffee.

Once a girl gave me a picture she had drawn. It was lovely. She was very excited to see me in school, I think. But she didn't tell me I looked better like she did last time. Maybe because I was so grumpy.

Actually I probably wasn't as grumpy then. How can you be grumpy when a girl gives you a pretty picture?

There is this thing that people do sometimes, where they hide a message in their writing using the first letter of every paragraph. So I just did it, but I am warning you, it is really lame. But I don't even care . . . so there.

No Sleep

I AM SERIOUSLY IN the most wacky, crazy mood ever. Sort of a cross between someone at a sleepover in the early hours of the morning and someone who has just been on a long, sleepless plane ride.

The cause for my weird mood is that I haven't slept in a long time. Once again I stayed up all night. And the results have been, well . . . strange.

Everything, even the most ordinary things, makes me laugh almost uncontrollably, which in turn is so weird it makes everyone else laugh.

I also have a weird sort of nervous energy. I just feel like tapping my cane on the floor over and over for no apparent reason. Now I'm tapping the keyboard instead. Pretty sweet.

Oh, and one more symptom. Dizziness. Dizziness. Weird.

There was something terribly interesting I was just going to say, but I forgot it so I will think of a new interesting thing to say. Oh, I just remembered the old interesting thing. I answered the phone at the same time as my mom. I did it on purpose too. I'm not sure why I did it. But I did, and it was my dad, and first he talked to me, but then he wanted to talk to my mom about something. I wanted to listen just to, you know, listen. So I listened, but I had a phone in one hand and a cane in the other hand. What does that have to do with anything? Oh yes, I wanted to put a cup in the sink. So I picked it up with my mouth and it fell out of course and banged around. I don't know why I'm saying this. I am not really thinking. I think my brain is half shut down. Maybe now you can feel sorry for my mom, because I already do.

A Real Narnia

YESTERDAY WAS ONE OF the rare occasions that I talked to my sister Amy on the phone. She told me about her students and things, and somehow, in some way, somebody got the bright idea that I could come visit her. I loved the idea of course, and so did she, and as soon as we hung up and Mom came home, I sprung it on her.

"Can I go to South Carolina and visit Amy for a week or so?"

Now I must backtrack and say that Mom has this thing about getting me to ask Dad things instead of asking her, since Dad is the one who always comes up with the best solutions to problems. So she said if I wanted to go, I needed to talk to Dad about it.

Then Mom had a talk with Dad. I didn't eavesdrop or anything, of course, but I'm pretty sure she told him I would love to take a trip to South Carolina, but that she wanted *me* to be the one to officially ask him.

Well, today I finally got up my courage and went into the living room, fully intending to ask Dad if I could. He sat up and looked at me expectantly.

It was weird how I felt then. Like I was staring at a glass box, with words floating and flying around and bumping into each other, yet I had no idea which ones to pull out of the box and use. Meanwhile Dad sat there, knowing the *exact* right words, just waiting for me to say them.

Finally Dad said, "Does it have to do with a plane trip?"

"Yes," I said.

"Does it have to do with a visit to the East Coast?"

"Yes," I said again. And then the words in the box settled down and I was able to choose the right ones from then on.

Dad told me that Mom wasn't sure I should go. He said Mom feels like she always has to push me to take my pills, and get up at a decent time in the morning, and work on my schoolwork. If I went to South Carolina, there would be no one to push me. If I could be responsible in those three areas for two weeks, they would look into sending me to South Carolina for a week and a half.

Wow. So many emotions. So much happiness. I feel like I've been living in a dungeon, and someone gave me a key and said, "Go through that door and down the hall, and you will end up in Narnia."

Narnia. South Carolina. What's the big difference? They

both have new things, and adventure, and people I've never met. I want to meet someone new! What is two weeks of being responsible? I can be responsible for two weeks if I have South Carolina dangling in front of me like a carrot on a string!

The only part that troubles me is the "week and a half" bit. I'm afraid I'll have an amazing time and then have to come home again.

But here's the thing. I have a certain feeling that Oregon is making me sick or maybe just this house, and if I go to South Carolina, I will start getting better. Then they'll have to let me stay longer, right?

I know that Dr. Hanson shooed away the idea that Oregon is making me sick and was quite positive I had West Nile. And I believe him, now, I guess. Whenever people ask, I say I have West Nile. Really, if you think about it, it makes sense. But I still cannot shake the idea that if I could just get away, I would get well.

And that is why South Carolina looms in front of me like a Narnia of sorts. That is why I still can't believe I really, truly, might be able to go.

Blessed

I AM BLESSED.

Now I know that is a horribly overused and clichéd thing to say, but I realized today it is true. I am blessed. Even though I'm sick and have no clue when I'll get better, even though I have virtually no social life, even though it's my senior year and I don't even know whether or not I'll manage to graduate, I'm still blessed.

So why am I blessed, you may ask?

I read a blog today, and the girl writing it seemed to be very depressed. She felt like she was lonely, ugly, unable to be herself around people, and without a boyfriend, which upset her greatly. She felt as though life was pointless, useless, and horrible.

This made me realize that although I do feel lonely at times, I get over it. And I can be myself around people. Well, okay, maybe not when I'm feeling horrible or have a severe lack of sleep, but it's not like I'm acting like someone I'm not. And furthermore, I'm not pining for a boyfriend. I can actually say that, at this point in my life, I am glad I don't have a boyfriend. Of course, I am only seventeen and officially too young to date. But seriously, there are lots of seventeen-year-olds pining for boyfriends. Even if they are officially too young to date. And I think the fact that this doesn't bother me in the least is a blessing.

Now I must say that life frequently seems pointless, useless, and horrible. I lie in bed, late at night, unable to sleep, and think about my life. And most often what I think about is how pointless, useless, and horrible it is. But honestly, I think it would be nearly impossible for someone in my circumstances to never get depressed.

The point, the reason I am blessed, is that I can get over my depression. I can wake up in the morning, determined to make the most of my life, no matter how pointless it is. I am sick, and it makes me depressed at times, but I would choose West Nile over being sick with depression. A million times.

Snow Day

I FELL ASLEEP LAST NIGHT to the comforting sound of rain on the roof and woke up to the less comforting but much more beautiful sight of falling snow. Lots of snow. Tons of snow. Mountains of snow. Enough snow that if you weren't too heavy, and if you went to a part of the yard that wasn't under a tree, you might be able to make a snow angel without green shoots of grass sticking up through it and ruining the effect.

And what do you know, it was enough snow that they canceled church. I can't remember the last time that happened.

The snow made Mom happy. Really happy. I don't know what it is about snow that lifts her mood so, because it doesn't really have that effect on me. Rain makes me happy, which is weird, because we get rain all the time and we hardly ever get snow.

So my mom and I were discussing rain and snow and happiness, which led into a discussion about whether we would rather get proposed to in the snow or in the rain. Mom didn't understand at all why I thought getting proposed to in the rain was romantic.

"But Mom," I said, "remember that scene from *Pride and Prejudice* when he proposed to her in the rain? Didn't you think that was romantic?"

Mom shuddered. "With the rain dripping off of his nose? You thought that was romantic?!"

Ben, Steven, and Jenny played in the snow. Mom went on numerous walks, made a gigantic snowman (seriously about as big as the snowmen Calvin is always building in *Calvin and Hobbes*), and just looked and looked and looked at the snow. Dad and I didn't feel like making ourselves cold, wet, and miserable, so we stayed inside.

That evening everybody sat down to play a game of Phase 10.

The game dragged on and on. When we finally finished, we realized it had taken us three hours. Wow.

It sounds kind of bad to say that you're glad church was canceled, but I really am. It's so cool to spend extra time with your family. Singing "I've been waiting for you all my life" from *George of the Jungle* whenever you get the exact card you needed, hearing your Dad accidentally say "I think I'll skip my mommy" instead of "I think I'll skip my wife," being constantly accused of being a "Peeker" by your brother after you just happen to see that he drew a wild card—those are the kinds of things that make great memories. Sometimes I think there is no one quite so fun to hang out with as your family.

Still More Randomness

SOMETIMES I THINK I could live off Dr Pepper and English muffins.

I just woke up, and it's 12:42 AM.

Tip for all of you out there who know someone who is really sick and don't know what to get them: get them an amaryllis bulb kit. Those things grow amazingly fast. It's so cool.

Why is it that everybody is always asking everybody else how they are doing? Seriously, the phrase *How are you doing?*

is getting to be about as common as *Hello*. And to say *Fine* back is just like saying *Hello* back when someone says *Hello* to you. It's an automatic response. Yet, how many people are actually doing *Fine?* Maybe some, but certainly not as many people as say they are, I don't think.

But what are you supposed to do when the clerk at the grocery store says, "How are you doing today?" Not that I've been to any grocery stores lately, but I remember stuff like that happening after Lenny died too. The grocery store clerk or some similarly out-of-my-life person would say, "How are you doing?" and I didn't know whether to lie and say "Fine," like they expected, or say, "Well, actually my cousin just committed suicide, and I'm doing horribly right now, thank you very much." Seriously. I think we need some new phrases.

Church and John McCane

I WAS RESPONSIBLE FOR two weeks. I also went to church last Sunday evening. It's freaky going to church, because everywhere you go there are people, people, people. They all look at me, and ask questions, and say "You look so great!"

At least that's how I was afraid it was going to be. But I had to go, because it was part of my test. How could I go to South Carolina if I couldn't even go to church?

I was super weak last Sunday. It usually takes me forever to go from point A to point B. Sometimes it takes me forever and ever. Last Sunday was one of those forever and ever days.

It is amazing to me how fast people walk. I never even thought about it until I became a weak, slow walker. But now I'm the first to leave the house and the last to get in the van. As I watch the others whizzing by me, walking at their normal pace, I think, *Wow. I used to walk that fast.* It just about blows my mind.

At church, everybody stared at me and talked to me, but no one said the dreaded, "You look so good!" I probably didn't look too good, shuffling along with my cane. It was a relief to actually look how I felt.

In church I sat, with no place to rest my head, and conversed with John McCane in my mind. There is something very comforting about John McCane. I squeeze him and tell him things (not out loud of course), and then he says something comforting back. It makes me feel like I'm not alone, even if I am.

Sometimes I wish I could forget that John McCane isn't real and actually believe he heard me and was talking back. There are other things I sometimes wish I could believe too, like that I'm a princess. You know, like crazy people in books. What is it like to go crazy? Is it fun? I bet it's not boring.

I can make up a personality for John McCane and pretend to talk to him. I can pretend I'm a princess. I can make up all sorts of things. Pretending is interesting and fun and comforting and perhaps childish, but being childish is better than being bored, I think. But it's just pretending.

But wait! I'm going to South Carolina where it's exciting for real! In just a little over a week! It's hard to believe something so lovely and exciting could actually be happening to me.

Tongue for Dinner

WE HAD A COW TONGUE for Sunday dinner. The thing had been sitting in the freezer for a long time, and Mom finally decided we might as well eat it.

I don't know about you, but to me, the idea of eating cow tongue is, well, revolting. My mom actually felt the same way. "The gross thing about it is that you put it in the frying pan and it looks just like, well, a tongue," she told me, shuddering. I took heart in the fact that I would probably not be forced to eat any.

The family sat around the table facing a Crockpot full of potatoes with a huge tongue hidden beneath them. Gingerly, Mom reached in, pulled out a section of tongue, and put it on Steven's plate. Jenny and I politely declined. Matt, however, seemed to think the idea of having tongue for Sunday dinner was cool.

Steven and Matt picked at their pieces of tongue. Jenny, Mom, and I just ate potatoes.

"How's the tongue, Matt?" asked Mom after a little while.

"Mmm-mm," said Matt.

Mom glanced at Matt and screamed. He had stuck his piece of cow tongue in his mouth, so it looked like he had a huge, gray disgusting tongue, and was sticking it out at Mom.

Jenny and I finally consented to trying cow tongue, as long as it was pealed first. If you take off the thick, gray, tastebud-ridden outer skin of the tongue, it doesn't look much different from a normal piece of meat. But it has a funny texture that I didn't like, so I only took one bite. Mom didn't eat any at all.

Most of the cow tongue got eaten by the dog, I think.

Wheelchair and Planes

JOHN MCCANE AND I flew to South Carolina. Everybody was looking at me as I walked by. Here I was, a seventeen-year-old Mennonite girl with a very bright skirt, a funny prayer veil on my head, and a cane. How often do you see that?

As soon as I was on the plane, I realized something I had never realized before flying with my family. It is extremely awkward to sit by strangers on a plane. You are so close to them, you feel like it is terribly rude not to talk to them. But you have no idea what to say.

I had to change planes in Atlanta. I walked out of that long hallway connecting the plane to the building, and then just stood there as people surged this way and that, rolling luggage along, chattering on their cell phones, and knowing where they were going. Where was I going? Oh sure, there was a letter and a number on my boarding pass telling me, but I didn't want to walk there. It was too far.

When we got my ticket we requested a wheelchair for me. Where was that wheelchair? Was it one of the three sitting off to the side with strong-looking guys standing behind them? Was I supposed to just go up to one of them and ask for a ride? Should I ask the lady behind the desk for help?

I was tired. I was hungry. I was confused. I was close to tears. I shouldn't have been close to tears. Stupid, stupid, stupid.

Have I ever told you of my strange fear of asking strangers for help? I wander around stores for ages trying to find things without ever asking the nice people with nametags for help. And perhaps I would have found the gate myself, slowly shuffling along, missed my flight, and burst into tears, if I hadn't caught the eye of one of the strong-looking guys behind the wheelchairs.

"Do you need a ride?" he asked, apparently noticing I was just standing there stupidly with my cane.

"Yes," I said gratefully. I sank wearily into the wheelchair.

And then we were off, pushing through the sea of people, cramming onto an elevator, and pushing through more people until we finally reached my gate. I switched from the blue wheelchair to the black airport chair. The strong wheelchair guy ran off.

On my way from Atlanta to Charlotte the flight attendant stood in the hallway, looked around, and said, "Is one of you Miss Smucker?"

"I am," I said.

"Did you request a wheelchair?" she asked.

I said I had. And when I stepped off the plane and into the Jetway, there was a wheelchair waiting for me, right there. But we waited and waited until pretty much everyone was gone before going back to the baggage claim.

And I couldn't get a hold of Amy.

When I got to baggage claim the guy behind the wheelchair said, "Do you see anyone you know ma'am?"

"No," I said, "I'll wait here until they get here."

As soon as he was gone I started crying.

Where was Amy? She didn't answer her phone. I called Dad. He didn't have any magic solution.

Another nice stranger came up to me. "Are you all right?" she asked.

I told her what was going on. She said comforting things to me.

And then Amy was there, telling me how sorry she was, that someone told her it took less time to get to the airport than it actually did, that her cell phone died. I dried my tears and collected my baggage and we were off, with me wanting to tell her all my flying adventures and her wanting me to shut up so she could concentrate on where she was going.

Just like old times.

Valentine's Day

IT SEEMS AS THOUGH every girl in the United States who does not have a significant other hates Valentine's Day. And yet I love it. Today, I got to wondering what it is that I love so much about Valentine's Day.

Maybe it's the valentines. I don't know why I love valentines, as they are never anything more than gestures of friendship, but who cares? I love them. They're so cute, and they indicate that you are special to someone, even if it's not some romantic significant other.

Maybe it's just the memories. It seems as though every Valentine's Day is full of good memories, whether it's making interesting and unique valentines for the whole school, making a valentine for Jesus and throwing it out a window like I did once when I was eight, or decorating heart-shaped cookies.

Or maybe it's something simple, like the fact that by Valentine's Day I am always over my winter sicknesses. In fact, this may be the first year I am sick on Valentine's Day, which is a weird thought.

This year, my Valentine's Day had the potential to be horrible, but in fact it was very lovely. I had an amazingly good day. I got to see my sister again, I met new people, and the weather was beautifully bright and sunny, but still nice and cool. And I did stuff, and while I didn't feel perfect, it was on the better side of things. It was the kind of day that makes me feel as though, maybe just maybe, I'm finally getting better.

Mitch

EVERY STORY AMY TELLS seems to be about her hilarious twelve-year-old student Mitch. Mitch did this funny thing. Mitch did that funny thing. Boy did I want to meet this Mitch. But for the first few days I was here, he was gone.

The day he returned was the day Amy and I did a skit for the students in chapel. Afterwards, they all had to file by and shake my hand. It was kind of weird.

"Did you meet Mitch?" Amy asked when it was over.

"Um, sort of," I said. "I shook his hand at least." He hadn't really seemed energetic and outgoing like I'd expected.

"Mitch! Come here!" Amy called. "Hey Mitch! Do you want to meet my sister?"

"We've already met!" he called over his shoulder and ran off.

He wasn't like I expected him to be at all. I was disappointed.

But wait! By the end of the day he apparently overcame his shyness of me. He sat by me and talked my ear off whenever possible. I loved every minute of it.

There are some people who think in such interesting ways that you can sit down and have a fascinating conversation with them without ever running out of things to say.

Mitch is one of those people.

Blisters and Sisters

A BLISTER HAS APPEARED on the bottom of my foot, making it difficult to walk. It is very odd.

Other than that, I feel better now than I have in months. Since about August, probably. I feel grand. The sun is shining, and the gravel is glittering, and if I don't try to throw anything or open any heavy doors, I can almost imagine what it's like to actually be in good health.

The only really bad day I've had since arriving was the first Sunday I was here. That was really weird because in the morning I didn't feel too bad, but then during praise and worship I got really weak and had to sit down. By the time praise and worship was over, I felt so bad that Amy had to take me home. I had to lean on the wall going out, since I didn't have my cane.

Last night at church this funny little old man came up to me and asked me how I was doing. "Are you better than last Sunday?" he asked.

I assured him that I was.

"You looked miserable," he said. "I thought you were blind."

I'm assuming the reason I looked blind was because I had my eyes half shut and I was leaning against the wall for support.

Anyway, besides that horrible Sunday when I felt sick and the old man thought I was blind, it has been going amazingly. Amy and I are doing all kinds of fun things, like having candlelit dinners with sparkling grape juice, watching movies, and of course talking and talking and talking.

To Leave or Not to Leave

I WAS SCHEDULED TO leave Monday, a week and a half after I got here. But all my theories turned out to be correct. I mean, since I've gotten here, I've felt great. So Mom and Dad will surely let me stay longer, right?

Wrong. It costs a lot of money to extend my stay. As for potentially moving out here for however long it takes to get me totally better or something, I didn't even bring it up.

But I don't want to leave. I mean, hello? *Every day* I go to school with Amy and help teach the kindergarten class. Every day I feel well enough to do this. Do you have any idea how amazing that is? And I get fresh air all the time because you can actually walk to places from Amy's home. Places like this amazing church that leaves its doors unlocked all the time, so you can go in and look at the beautiful green carpets and benches and the purple and yellow stained-glass windows. It is so beautiful and reverent that it amazes me.

And then there's Mitch, who never fails to do something interesting. And Amy, who is super, of course.

But mainly I *feel* so good, and I don't want it to stop. Isn't it worth a little extra money to make me feel healthier and stronger? I haven't used John McCane *once* since I got here!

Boy, was I mad at my parents. I wanted to say, "Hello? Look at me! Don't I look happy? Don't I look well? Don't you want me to look happy and well?"

Then I got the call saying, "Oh, we found a better deal, you can stay until Saturday."

Yay!

Pros: I get to stay longer! A whole week almost! I get to go to the cool February 29th party Amy's students are putting on!

Cons: I still have to leave.

But I'm going to make the most of it. When I get home I'll tackle my schoolwork with a vengeance. If I'm too sick to go with my family to Kenya in April, I'll go to South Carolina instead and hang out with Amy some more. That's two weeks right there.

I'll be back.

The Smart Mouse

ONE NIGHT, AS I WAS calmly standing around in the kitchen I saw a mouse run down the hall.

I shrieked (of course), Amy came running (of course), and we looked for it (of course), but we couldn't find it (of course). The worse part was that it was in one of the bedrooms. I was imagining waking up to find a mouse in my hair or something, but thankfully that never happened. In fact, there seemed to be no trace whatsoever of the mouse.

Ruth, Amy's landlady, set a mousetrap for us in our laundry room (actually it's more of a laundry closet). But a few days went by and not even a trace of a mouse appeared.

Then there came a day when we opened the door to the garbage closet and there were mouse turds on the floor. We got Esther, Amy's roommate, to move the mousetrap from the laundry closet to the garbage closet because we were afraid we would get our fingers snapped.

The next day, the cheese was gone, but the trap had not sprung.

We let it go for a few days, but finally we decided the trap needed some peanut butter on it instead of cheese. So we carefully scraped peanut butter onto the trap using wooden chopsticks, trying not to snap our fingers.

The next day, the peanut butter was gone, and the trap still had not sprung.

"I wonder if it actually *can* spring," I asked Amy.

"I don't know," said Amy. "Why don't you try it?"

I grabbed the broom to spring the mousetrap with, but while doing so I accidentally knocked over the mop bucket, which fell on top of the mousetrap and sprung it.

"Well, I guess now we know it works," I said.

Unfortunately, that knowledge didn't do us much good, as both Amy and I are scared to set the mousetrap again because it might snap on our fingers. Esther and Ruth are gone. And plus, there isn't much point in resetting the mouse trap anyway, because it is obvious the mouse is far smarter than we are.

February 29

PEOPLE SET UP LIGHTS, flowers, tablecloths, and candles in one end of the gym. Students practiced singing and playing their instruments. Everyone was preparing for the February 29th party, which the students were putting on for parents and people in the church as a fundraiser.

I just sat around videotaping and talking to Mitch.

We went home for a bit to change, and when we got back it was totally enchanting. The lights had been turned off, and candles and strings of twinkle lights glittered around the room. Everyone was all dressed up. Mitch had a black tie with little airplanes on it, and suspenders. Everybody loved the suspenders.

Mitch came up to me and bowed. "May I have this dance?"

"I'd be delighted, young man," I said with a curtsy.

The "dance" only lasted several seconds. As you may have gathered from the fact that I said, "I'd be delighted, young man," the only dancing I know how to do is what I've seen in movies and tried to imitate.

At this point I was thinking it was going to be quite the enchanted evening. But I was wrong. Because everyone had something to do except me. The girls prepared food and served it. The guys valet parked the cars except for Mitch, who is only twelve or so. He escorted the ladies inside.

But me? I sat around like an idiot until Shela, the only senior girl, handed me her camera and asked if I could take pictures for her. She was too busy. That was a bit unnerving, because she is a great photographer, and I am a horrible one. But at least it was something to *do*.

Then it was over, and people cleaned up, and we left. Yep, that was it. And tomorrow I'm leaving South Carolina.

But I'll be back.

Right?

March 2008

Home Again

REMEMBER HOW MY greatest fear about going to South Carolina was coming back? Turns out it was a valid concern.

Nothing is new under the sun. I never thought I had anything resembling seasonal affective disorder (SAD) until I got back. Everything looks depressing. There is no sun, and there is no due west, and there are no breathtaking churches with purple and yellow stained-glass windows and benches covered in green velveteen.

As for the people, there is no Mitch.

I have been so lazy since returning. I had hoped I would be able to tackle working for Mom in full force, but it turns out I am still far too lazy. Laziness is a horrible thing to have. And yet, I didn't really seem to struggle with it in South Carolina.

It seems as though all I have been doing since I got back is complaining. I don't know why. But I just can't seem to get my life together like I had hoped.

Hyperventilating

I HIT THE GROUND RUNNING when I came home. Went to church Sunday, and though I skipped Monday, I went to school Tuesday, Wednesday, and Thursday, getting tests over with and out the door.

Thursday was when everything began to unravel.

Thursday was music class. I didn't wanna go. I haven't gone since September. But I figured now I would have to go back, since I was hoping to be in school pretty much full-time from now on.

The first thing we needed to do, said Jean, the music teacher, was run laps around the church parking lot.

"I can't run!" was my panicked cry. Only I was too embarrassed to make it audible to anyone besides the people right next to me.

"You can walk," said Bethany.

So I walked. I walked slowly. I got tired, breathless, weak, but I wasn't even halfway around. On I pressed.

And when I finally made it I felt a little silly that I was weak as can be from such a short walk.

Then I sat down for music. I was fine. I got over my lack of breath from the walk. And then we started singing.

A verse or two later, I was out of breath again. So I rested, and then I sang again. And I rested and sang. But when I began to feel lightheaded, I stopped singing altogether.

When we switched songs I turned the page, but I didn't sing. The lightheaded pangs didn't go away. They spread, sending secret shocks throughout my body. When we switched songs again, I found I didn't want to turn the page. So I didn't, and then I told myself to, so I did.

By the time we switched to another song, I couldn't turn the pages. My body would not respond anymore.

And there I sat.

Felicia said, "Are you all right?"

I couldn't look at her. I couldn't answer her. I hoped she would figure out that something was wrong, but she didn't.

The clock. I had to see what time it was. Go up, I told my eyes. Slowly, jerkily, they moved upward. Now to the left, I commanded them. They didn't want to obey. But I told them to, and in slow jerky motions, they focused on the clock on the wall. Five minutes. Five minutes until everyone would leave, everyone but me, and they would realize something was wrong.

My heart beat harder, faster. I looked at the other students, and it was as though I was in a bubble. They went on looking and acting and singing like everything was normal, but there in my bubble, nothing was normal anymore. It was like they were in a totally different world than I was—like I was watching a movie about them, and nothing they could do would affect me.

It was all so scary and sad that the tears I was trying to hold back slipped down my cheeks.

I breathed in, but no air came.

I gasped in desperation.

At that moment, the bubble burst. People turned around, and began yelling, "Open the window! Go get Mr. Smucker! Get her outside!"

Someone hauled me outside. Someone else got a chair. And whether they hung around for a while or went back to the classroom, I don't know, because all I could think of was the fact that I could not breathe.

Slowly I calmed down, and began to breathe more easily. My palms tingled. I began to tremble. I needed to get back to the classroom and finish my test. I was better now. Slightly weakened, but better.

I slept as soon as I got home. All evening and all night was spent on the couch with a small blanket, in my clothes, sleeping, then waking up, then sleeping.

And ever since then, I've felt horrible. It's like I took a gigantic step forward when I went to South Carolina, and then when I hyperventilated I took another step the same size, only it was backwards.

Strange.

The Dream

I JUST HAD A DREAM (I woke up in the middle of it, and now I'm writing this) that I will share with you.

Everything was going wrong for me. I was sick and weak—seriously, why can't I be nice and healthy in my dreams?—so weak that I collapsed onto the floor and couldn't get up. Then all of a sudden I realized I was wearing very little clothing. I was so embarrassed that I threw a blanket around my shoulders and ran.

There were a bunch of people outside, and I was so upset that I started singing to them. First I sang about how I always stood out in the crowd because I'm a Mennonite girl. Then I sang about how boring and bleak and horrible my life was because I was so sick, and how going to this youth retreat (so I guess I was at a youth retreat, though I had been hanging out with Tinkerbell in my dorm, so I'm not sure . . .) was supposed to be all wonderful and exciting, but more horrible things had happened there. My point was that I was running away from it all because I was so tired of it.

But the awesome thing about it was that it was just like I was in a musical or something. You know, background music mysteriously appeared, and I had a good voice all of a sudden.

I've made up songs as I went along in real life before, but I don't think I've ever done it in a dream.

Anyway, I was running away as I sang, since that's what I was singing about. I ran and ran, but it was too good to last. I collapsed, of course, but at least I got to run. I haven't been able to do that in real life for about six months. Anyway, the last verse of song was all about how I was out of breath and was probably going to hyperventilate. I was lying on the ground, exhausted, but there was a small group of people who had followed me, all strangers, and they gathered around me. I had the feeling they really cared about me and were going to help me. And then I woke up.

Going Nowhere

AM I DESTINED TO go nowhere in life?

I did get to go to South Carolina. But there was another thing I was looking forward to, and all of a sudden I can't go. My Sunday school class was going to go to Eagle Crest for the weekend. I haven't hung out with my friends in ages, and Eagle Crest sounds like an awesome resort even though I've never been there. But now there's too much snow in the passes. We can't go.

That, by itself, I can get over. But pair that with the Kenya trip and am I destined to go nowhere in life?

I was thirteen when we went to Kenya the first time. Unfortunately, it was during one of those weird lulls where I didn't keep a diary. But I remember feelings I had while I was there, and read odd bits I scribbled down in notebooks, and it is fascinating. I want to go back. I want to experience it again.

Our family has all these plans to fly to Kenya again this April. We weren't sure we could, for a while, because there was all this fighting over there. But then the two guys who both wanted to be president signed some sort of agreement, and everything is fine and peachy. So we're planning to go after all.

Everyone but me.

My dad has this idea there's a chance I'll get a little better and be able to go. But not me. Or my mom. Because going to Kenya is a big trip, not a little one like going to South Carolina. And even if I could somehow handle it, there is so much disease in Kenya. I mean, what if I got something else on top of West Nile? What would it do to me?

I thought maybe Amy wouldn't be able to get off school for two weeks to go to Kenya, and I could stay with her over that time. But it's not gonna happen. She got off. Everyone is going but me.

Pink Jelly Beans and CPR

THERE IS ONE THING I don't understand about life, and that is jellybeans. Especially pink jellybeans. How can something look so cute and have such a cute name, and yet taste so gross?

I guess it's just one of those things that looks good and tastes awful, like lipstick or daffodils. I don't know of anyone who's ever eaten lipstick before. And I guess I don't actually know what daffodils taste like, only that they are poisonous. I heard about a lady who decided daffodils were so pretty that she was going to make a soup out of them. It killed most of her family, including herself.

That story was told to us as a cautionary tale in the first aid/CPR class we had to take today. So besides knowing never to eat daffodil soup, even if all your friends are doing it, I also learned to do CPR on a dummy I named Christine.

We also learned mouth to mouth, which wasn't as weird as I thought it was going to be. The dummy didn't really have a face, just a hole in its head that you stuffed a plastic bag into for a lung. Then everyone had their own personal rubber dummy face that snapped on, as well as a breathing barrier, so you weren't breathing directly into their mouth but into the breathing barrier.

But I still find the idea of mouth to mouth gross, so if you're planning on having a near-death experience any time soon and want me to rescue you, I would rather you be choking.

Day

I WENT TO CHURCH ON Sunday, but in the evening I did not feel up to par. *Should I go to the youth group thing? Should I go home?* The questions reverberated in my head.

Justin walked in. "What's up?" he asked.

"I'm trying to decide whether or not to go to the youth thing," I said.

"Hmm," said Justin, "let's list the pros and cons." He started listing all sorts of pros, but whenever I mentioned a con he tried to shoot it down. Then others started gathering around. J. D. offered to wear his red shoes if I would come. Heath offered to take me home. So finally I said, "Okay . . . fine."

"Come with us. We're leaving right now," said Justin, pushing me forward. I had to go tell Mom first, but once we were on our way, Justin, J. D., and I had a great time chatting.

The party was horrible and wonderful. My headache was brutal and the noise was overpowering, but everyone was so nice and funny. I was glad I had come. Sometimes excitement is worth pain.

I have been doing lots of stuff lately, it seems, like going to school every once in a while, or church or a youth thing, but I still feel sick. Sometimes I wonder if those feelings will ever go away.

I guess if I can live in the moment and trust in God, everything will be fine.

Night

I AM SUCH A LOSER.

Look at me. Look at my life. I'm graduating. I'm turning eighteen. I'm sick. Nothing is sound anymore. I can't just live anymore. I can't just make the best of what I have because I don't have anything anymore.

I am losing the chance to go to Kenya, losing it every day. And every day I think of new things, things I did and saw when I was there last time that I may never do and see again.

I want someone to tell my troubles to. At night, when everything rushes down on me, I know I must tell someone. But there is no one to tell.

Is all lost?

Right now I'm thinking maybe I should learn to do that cool thing they do in movies where they scream so loud all the glass breaks. Or maybe they sing really high and screechy but I don't feel like singing high and screechy. I feel like screaming so loud all the glass breaks. How awesome would that be?

Day and Night

EVERY DAY I CAN shove my problems aside and enjoy the good things life hands me, even if I am in pain.

Every night I cry in anguish because life seems so hopeless.It seems to never end.

April 2008

Sinking Down

I AM ON A SERIOUSLY annoying downward spiral. I feel icky all the time again. Really icky. So all I do is sit at home all day watching movies and surfing the Internet on Mom's laptop for excitement, occasionally dreaming up things or watching rainbows dance in my eyelashes.

For about a whole week I cried every night. Deep, deep into the night when no one is awake, I would sob to myself, because life was horrid. Pointless. Insanely pointless. Nothing I did mattered. Nothing. And I couldn't go anywhere because of how horrible I felt. But I don't cry at night so much now.

I began writing simple blog posts about how I felt like screaming and stuff, because I was so mad at life but couldn't bring myself to out-and-out complain on my blog.

Then one night I went to bed early and woke up at one in the morning. I got on and what do you know—Shelley, my cousin Randy's girlfriend, had written me a comment asking what I felt like screaming about. Which was exactly what I was hoping someone would ask.

I wrote her a big, long, complaint-filled message. After all, she had *asked* why I felt like screaming. Then I sent it and went to sleep feeling much, much, better.

She replied saying wonderful things. All the nice things I hoped she would say and more. After that I didn't cry to the night nearly as much. But I began to feel sicker and sicker, which could be part of it, because sometimes my brain is too shot to even despair.

So here I am. It is late, and I feel horrible, body and brain. It feels like this setback is here to stay. And I will lie in bed forevermore.

Sometimes it feels like when my brother stomps up the stairs singing "When I was sinking down" in his really loud, low dramatic voice, he is personally tapping into something in me that is very raw. I want to shut out the world while I sink down. I want to lie still and dream of the beautiful things and the confusing prospects of life. I don't want anyone to talk to me, and the light needs to be turned off. I wish it was later, and no one would invade. No noise. No movement. And I could look out the window at the stars and sing the song in my heart, and no one would ever know.

Nothing at All

I DIDN'T WANT TO STAY HOME while my family was in Kenya. I wanted to have a mini-adventure, like going to South Carolina with Amy, only of course that didn't work out. So Mom posted about it on her blog and called relatives, and somehow we worked out this complicated plan.

First I'll be spending several days with Uncle Fred and Aunt Loraine in Oklahoma. The rest of the time I'll be in Kansas.

Wait, Kansas? Who do I know in Kansas?

Well . . . no one. But a friend of Mom's thought I should stay with Mom's aunt and uncle (whom I've never met) who live there. Only that didn't work out, so she found alternate housing for me nearby, with families from the church who have daughters relatively close to my age.

One of the families I've never heard of before. The other family is, of all things, the Mast family. The famous Mast family.

What makes them famous? They're just an ordinary family from Kansas, but my mom reads their blogs and is intrigued by them. She talks about them like she knows them. That's why the idea of meeting the Masts seems like meeting someone famous, because I hear about them all the time but never expected to meet them.

So how do I feel about the trip? Of course a small part of me is disappointed. I should be going to Kenya with my family and the other seniors in my class. Kenya is certainly more exciting and exotic than Kansas, that I am quite sure of. But it is also more disease-ridden. That is the last thing I need right now.

I should be scared too. I'll know my relatives in Oklahoma of course, but in Kansas I will know no one. What if they have a depressing house with dark walls, dead animal heads everywhere, and hardly any books? What if the people I stay with get on my nerves? What if I feel horrible and don't have anyone I know around to comfort me? What if the house smells weird? But for some reason I'm not scared anymore. I was, but now I'm not, and I'm not sure why.

But most of all I really should be excited. My life is so lifeless and boring; something like this should send me into frenzies of elation. When I heard I was going to South Carolina, I could hardly contain my joy. So why am I not more excited than I am?

I'm feeling nothing at all. It's weird to feel nothing when you should be feeling something.

Never Mind

OKAY, I'LL ADMIT IT, I didn't want to go. I don't know why, but I didn't want to. I didn't want them to go, either. I wanted everyone to stay home and wait for me to get better, and then we could go to Kenya together.

Well, all I can say is, be careful what you wish for.

One hour before we were going to leave, I checked my brother Matt's blog. Matt isn't going to Kenya with them. Did I mention that? He's away at school.

"Pray for my family," Matt said on his blog. "They are on their way *here*." I clicked on the indicated link and up popped an article about more violence cropping up in Kenya. Apparently, thinking we were already on our way, he hadn't bothered to call us about it.

"Mom," I said running downstairs. "Mom, I have to show you something."

She read it. She called Dad. Dad called people.

The verdict? No Kenya.

Which also means no Kansas. As soon as I heard that, I desperately wanted to go. Especially when Heidi Mast, the middle child of the famous Mast family, commented on my blog and said:

Emily, I was really sorry to hear that you aren't coming here after all! I'm Heidi from Kansas, and you were gonna stay with me for a few days and then with one of my friends for a few more . . . and lol, I can assure you that we don't have dead animal heads decorating our house, and I hope it's not dark and depressing! My sister is addicted to books so that shouldn't have been a problem . . . I have some food allergies myself, and when Mom was reading me yours I was thinking how much fun it would be to make you special meals. =) There's a group of us girls out here that were eagerly awaiting your arrival and think you sound like a blast! We were planning for a while all the amazing things we were gonna do while you were here—if you're feeling good enough. We had a drama picked out to do, parties in the hayloft, reading some of our favorite books out loud to you, etc. I think you're hilarious, and I love reading your posts! Anyway, us girls would love to have you come sometime anyway, even if your family's not going to Kenya . . . just want to let you know you're always welcome!

Of course I wanted to go more than anything after that, but it was too late.

And now, everyone is so disappointed about Kenya and I'm thinking, *Why did I wish for this? Am I crazy?* It's one of those times when it's really nice to know that somehow God has a plan all figured out. Seriously.

Every Ant Must Die

I WAS IN MY BEDROOM making tea. Everybody else was asleep. Blindly, I reached down to get a sugar cube.

I pulled out the box of sugar cubes. It was swarming with ants. Now I don't hate ants like I hate moths, but when there are ants swarming over something I just can't stand it. They simply must die.

Normally, I could bribe my brothers to do such a task, but my brothers were currently sleeping away.

The annoying thing about ants is that they are hard to kill. Seriously. You can squish them, of course, but then they stink and several ants might crawl up your arm by the time you have squished one. And it takes forever to drown an ant.

I sprayed the whole box liberally with all-purpose cleaner from the bathroom. Some of then shriveled up and died, while others walked around like nothing had happened. And still more ants kept climbing out from between the cubes.

Well. Back to the bathroom I went, this time getting the old plastic container that the toilet brush sits in and filling it with water. The whole box of sugar cubes got dumped into this. Then I carried the whole contraption back to the bathroom, where I squirted little piles of lotion over any ant that dared to climb to the top of the box, out of the water.

That'll show those ants who they're messing with.

And by the way, mint tea really doesn't taste that bad without sugar.

Alternate Vacation

THERE IS NOTHING QUITE LIKE cramming six people into a pop-up tent-trailer for a weekend. For one thing, everybody pretty much has to go to bed and wake up at exactly the same time, because the slightest movement vibrates the whole flimsy contraption and wakes up everyone else. I got around this rule by reading with the light from my cell phone after hours and going back to sleep every time someone woke me up the next morning. But the latter gave me strange dreams, all about my mom yelling at me to get up, chasing me all over the bed trying to whack me with a folding chair, and telling me I had hairs growing on my chin. I was so mad I woke up yelling, causing everyone else to laugh. It turns out that in reality Mom had been telling Ben that hairs were growing on his chin.

Most of the meals were eaten outside, due to the nice weather and the cramped living spaces indoors. But breakfast was eaten inside, with everyone stepping over boxes, trying to convert the bed into a table, dipping tea out of a pan into ugly plastic cups with a ladle that tended to drip.

But even with everything so cramped inside, it was really beautiful outside. And there is something adventurous about spending time camping in a little trailer with your family.

The reason we went camping was to have a little fun, even though Kenya got canceled. And it worked. It wasn't amazingly adventuresome, as I spent a lot of time just lying down in the camper, but it was still fun.

Like, that evening I followed the sandy trails all the way to the end, at the outskirts of town. I walked to the bridge, and then sat there, amazed I had walked so far. When did I get so much energy? I haven't used John McCane since I got home from South Carolina, but I still haven't been particularly strong.

I called Dad. He picked me up. I think he was annoyed with me for not coming back before dark but at the same time proud of me for walking so far.

All in all it was a lovely little vacation. It felt great. I read good books. I hung out with my family. What more could I ask for?

Three Quirky Habits

1. I have a habit of sitting in church and trying to position myself exactly right so it looks like the preacher is in the ear of the person in front of me.

2. Usually when I settle down to read I take my hair down to get more comfortable. Then I take whatever was holding my hair up and fiddle with it while I read. I use my hair chopsticks to poke myself with, and if they are translucent I place them over the line I'm reading and try to read through them. I clip hairclips onto the book and onto each other and onto my fingers.

3. I tend to do a lot of strange things to occupy my time when I'm in the car, since I'm usually not driving. Since before I can remember I've always imagined a long knife jutting out from the side of the car and cutting down all the grass and trees and bushes and signs along the road as we drove along. Sometimes I just pretended that the car's shadow was a knife. Whenever I'm seated just behind the driver and it's dark, I try to situate my head so I can't see the oncoming car's headlights. They are always blocked by the driver's head. Then, when the driver's head starts to glow, I try to time myself exactly right so I quickly close my eyes, the car zooms past, and then I open them without ever seeing the car's direct headlights.

So there you have it.

Unmentioned Amazingness

THERE ARE THOSE WHO are so wonderful, so self-sacrificing, yet I never mention them. Why? Every day I should write of their amazingness.

How can I even begin to describe how beautiful my mom is? I complain, and she listens. Weeks go by. Months. Years could pass, and she would not change. She would still bring me tea on lovely little trays. She would still feel sorry for me when I complained. She would still do anything in her power to help me. Can you imagine a more beautiful soul?

And my dad. He always says, "Emily! You look so well!" It's quite discouraging, until I look in his eyes and see how desperately he wants me to get better. Normally he is very careful about saving money, but I believe he would pay anything if it would help me feel better. He pays for countless blood tests and doctor visits. When our family went to the coast for the weekend and I felt good, he was talking of taking me to the coast *every* weekend, if it would help.

But most of all it's God. Why does it feel like it would cheapen an unbelievably beautiful relationship if I blabbered on and on about Him? Yet why does the single most important thing in my life get left out of my writings so often?

How can I describe what God does for me? How can I

explain the cold and lonely nights when I have nothing, nothing at all, but Him? When he says, "I have a plan," how can I describe the hope it brings, even though I can't see a faint semblance of anything good ever coming from this?

Yet I know He is telling the truth.

I trust Him. How can I not? He took my worries away.

Prize Capsule Machine

REMEMBER HOW I TALKED ABOUT the Mast family? It turns out that the oldest one, Hans, is currently in Oregon. He came to a church potluck, and we stood in line together. "Where are your brothers?" he asked.

You know those things at stores that look like gumball machines only they have prize capsules with interesting things in them, but when you put the quarter in and turn the handle, out pops a prize capsule with some cheap plastic doohickey in it that you don't even want? That's how my brain was right then. There are a million interesting answers to "Where are your brothers?" You could say "They flew off to Neverland," or "They ate too much food, grew two inches, and now they're hiding because they're embarrassed about how short their pants are" or even "I think I saw the Pied Piper go by a few minutes ago, maybe they followed him."

But of all the interesting answers to pop out, it had to be, "Oh, they died."

I'm serious. That's what I said. "Oh, they died." He snickered slightly to be polite, since I was obviously trying to be funny, but I wanted to sink to the floor. Because, if you think about it, it was not interesting or funny at all. It was actually rather morbid.

Stupid prize capsule-machine brain.

May 2008

Skip Day

EVERY YEAR THE juniors take the seniors on a surprise overnight trip, skipping a day of school. Only this year the sophomores took us, because there are no juniors.

I always imagined my skip day to be like this: Me, Justin, and Bethany walk out of school, suspecting nothing. All of a sudden the sophomores go, "Hey guys, guess what, it's Skip Day!"

"Skip Day?" we gasp in surprise and astonishment as our moms drive up and hand us bags of clothes they packed for us. Then we all pile into a van and drive to some exotic place we never would have imagined going, where we have so many fun times it is impossible to count them.

Wanna know what really happened?

A week ago Mom said, "Emily, you don't know this, but you might want to pack your bags."

Sure enough, last Friday I was lying in bed feeling awful when Stephy called. "Hey guess what? It's Skip Day!" she said. "We'll pick you up at your house soon."

I waited and waited. Then they arrived and Ben came running upstairs, frantically throwing things into his backpack. I went to the van. Turned out the reason they got here so late was because they also had to pick up Justin and Bethany. Bethany was at work. Justin was sick too. It was the first Skip Day ever that none of the seniors were in school.

Everything was wrong. I was sick. Justin was sick. The whole trip yielded only one halfway interesting conversation. I shot a decent movie with my video camera about monsters in closets, and did a funny acting game with the other girls. Other than that? Sickness. Headache. Watching other people have fun. I mean ick.

Most of the day I spent lying down at the beach house, while everyone else ran around in the sand and played football, and went shopping, and did all sorts of fun stuff. I mean, I sort of feel like I was cheated out of a decent Skip Day, you know?

The Room

EVER SINCE MATT moved out, his room has just been sitting there empty until Dad has enough time to redo it into a marvelous paradise for me. I've been waiting for that day since I was thirteen, and soon it will be here!

Dad dry-walled it and hired a guy to come spread this white stuff all over the walls to smooth them out. I picked out the most enchanting green paint called "Shimmering Lime," but I wasn't strong enough to paint it myself, so we asked a lady from church who loves to paint if she could do it for us.

Now it's painted and all it needs are finishing touches and furniture and things like that. Steven finally started working on the ceiling today, filling the holes with something white. He stood on boards, which rested on sawhorses. Jenny loved the boards, riding them like horses and naming them horse names. I don't know why she called the boards her horses instead of the sawhorses, but then again, who can know the ways of Jenny?

I can't wait to move in! I've been trying to think of a good name for my new room. I considered "Tara" from *Gone with the Wind*, but it's too short and abrupt and not quite lovely enough.

Yearbook

ONE OF THE SEVERE DISADVANTAGES of being sick for the entire school year and being editor of the yearbook at the same time is that, as you may guess, it is very difficult to get the yearbook completed on time. Justin is the only other one who really knows how to do anything, and he can't make any final decisions without me.

Yesterday, Bethany, Justin, and I worked on the yearbook, staying after school and actually working a total of eight straight hours. Today it was only four. We got it done. All the yearbook pages are put together!

Tomorrow I will graduate. Mom bought me silver pumps. I can't decide if I like them or not. But I suppose I will wear them anyway. My silver dress is done, and so is my green jacket.

I finished my speech tonight. I have a distant pleading hope that it will be something lovely people will remember, something that will touch people, something that will make people see something, I'm not sure what. But I want *something* to come out of this. I mean, I'm not even really graduating.

I suppose since I was such a unique case, being sick the entire school year, the school board was lenient on me. I'm graduating, getting a fake diploma, and then finishing up the rest of my stuff at home.

So here I am, graduating, leaving school forever. And yet it doesn't feel like I'm leaving school forever because it feels like I already left school forever, a long time ago. For the first two weeks of school, between West Nile's first kick and his second, I felt like I was a part of school. Ever since then, every time I've gone back I've felt like I was just a visitor.

I peeked into the fellowship hall this afternoon. Shiny silver tablecloths with black graduation hats printed on them covered the tables. A huge poster was hung over the ugly window between the fellowship hall and the old kitchen, with something graduation-like written on it. And there were white and green daisies in pretty vases.

I hope that graduation will turn out well.

Graduation

GRADUATION WAS LIKE I ordered a chocolate cake and got something else instead, maybe a pickle. A really good, fat, juicy pickle. It wasn't chocolate-cakelike at all.

The auditorium was unbearably hot. The whole time J. D. was up there giving us an amazing speech about holding onto our dreams or something, I was afraid I was going to hyperventilate. I barely heard any of it. Amy brought me a glass of water and Bethany fanned me, and then went out to tell someone to turn the thermostat down.

Then it was time to give my speech. I was seriously freaked out about it. I mean, I was talking about my sickness because I couldn't very well talk about the school year, since I hardly was in school. The problem was, there is no good ending to my story.

My mom helped me write it. I told her all about the

frustrations of being sick, missing out on life, and being uncertain of my future. She took notes. Then I stopped talking. I had no more to say.

"However . . ." she prompted.

Then I burst out with the main thing that was wrong with my story. "There are no howevers! I feel like everybody will expect me to say, 'However, all these wonderful character-building things came out of this so it was all worthwhile.' But in my mind there are no howevers yet! I still feel sick, and I don't think I've changed into some sort of wonderful patient person or anything like that. I don't understand why I have to go through this!"

"Then say that," my mom told me.

So I did. With everybody watching me, expecting me to talk about the special grace from God I received during my time of sickness, or about the amazing things I learned from it, or about something good that came from the pain, I told them the truth.

"I always believed before this sickness came that God would never give me more than I could handle. But I realized during this time that the big flaw in that is we can handle anything if we're not given a choice. We think there are things we can't handle . . . we'd just go crazy. But if something is handed to you, you just get through it if you think you can or not, because going crazy is a lot harder than it sounds.

"I can't say I ever got mad at God, or that I ever felt like He deserted me, I just don't understand, I still don't understand, so many things. I don't understand why I had to get sick in the first place. I don't understand why it had to be my senior year. I don't understand why it had to last so long. But most of all, I don't understand why I didn't get this outpouring of grace to go through this hard time like it seemed all those other people who have gone through hard times got."

My speech ended. I could see people, and they looked moved. Bethany discreetly brushed tears away. Justin told me, in a serious voice, that he thought I had done well. It gave me a fluttery feeling of happiness inside.

Afterwards many people told me just that. They loved my speech. They also congratulated me on graduating, which I didn't understand, since all I got was a fake diploma.

I opened piles of presents and talked, and opened more presents and talked, and finally, I was exhausted. I went home then. And that was it. The end. I left so early that no one even got a picture of the complete graduating class.

It was a nice enough graduation—I got presents and people liked my speech. But it was pickle nice, not chocolate cake nice.

Epic Randomness

SO FAR, THE MOTHS have stayed pretty much out of my way this year. I was beginning to think with some happiness that perhaps I had killed them all off last year. Not so, apparently. I saw a moth yesterday, but unfortunately I lacked the strength to go chasing after it. Steven, the moth rights activist around here, would be so proud.

I am tired of pills, pills, and more pills. Why does everyone think they have the magic pill that will cure me? Why do I have to try them all out?

Amy is home now, which means I have to move from her couch to my bed. Sometimes I wonder why couches are so much more comfortable than beds. But anyway, it's super having a big sister again.

Colorado

IN THE BOONDOCKS of Colorado, five-and-a-half hours from the nearest reasonably priced airport and somewhere around twenty hours from here, my cousin was getting married. Matt, Mom, Dad, Jenny, and I crammed in the car and drove to the wedding, every seat filled. Needless to say, it was a little squished.

We left at 3:30 PM, drove through the night, and arrived around noon. It seemed like all anyone wanted to do the whole trip was sleep. And somehow, none of us could. It was particularly hard for me, Mom, and Jenny, in the back seat. After all sorts of maneuvering and whining, Jenny finally put her head in Mom's lap and her feet in mine, and slept like a baby. But Mom and I, with our laps full of Jenny, couldn't get into a comfortable position to save our lives. And every time I shifted around I seemed to stick my fingers in someone's hair or poke someone else's toe.

Finally we arrived in Colorado, took nice naps, and then went to the rehearsal dinner. It was a strange rehearsal dinner. Neither the bride nor the groom were there.

The next day was the wedding. Matt got bored and drew the back of Grandma's head on his bulletin. I briefly met the bride's sister, who had candida for almost a year and so knows what it's like to have a long prolonged sickness, but I didn't get to talk to her much. I left the reception early since I wasn't feeling well, and the rest of the day I just hung out with my family and my Aunt Barb and my cousin Stephy.

Sunday morning, we all piled into our car to come home. Jenny was in a singing mood. She sang "How much wood would a woodchuck chuck" over and over, and when I asked her to stop she sang "Goo goo ga ga goo ga goo" to the same tune. She sang "If my brother told a lie, I could see it in his eye," which is a silly song I made up, only she sang it wrong, which drove me nuts. Then Mom bought her a cowboy hat at a gas station, since Jenny is all into horses, and after that Jenny attempted to sing Patch the Pirate songs with a country twang.

Nothing would make her stop. She would feel bad for annoying everyone, stop singing for about five minutes, and then start up again, repeating the song she'd been singing for the last two hours. Finally Matt decided to let her listen to his iPod. He was quite proud of himself, wondering why he hadn't thought of that solution earlier. But then Jenny started singing "mmm mmmmm in Texas, you gotta have a fiddle in the band." She mumbled the words she didn't know and sang some notes way too high and others way too low. Needless to say, it didn't exactly solve the singing problem.

This time, when we got to Salt Lake City, we dropped Dad off so he could fly home. That gave us much more room.

Slowly it got darker and darker, and Mom and Jenny fell asleep. I stayed awake to help keep Matt awake and to watch for deer. We drove and drove, and talked about Bigfoot in whispers, scaring ourselves good and proper. The desert road at night is a truly enchanting thing. And then we began seeing less and less sagebrush and more and more trees, and we were in the beautiful part of Oregon again, and I dropped off to sleep.

One More Test

I HAVE A SECRET WISH that there is something in Oregon's environment that's making me sick. I want to move and get better, and have an exciting life somewhere else. That's what I've wanted ever since I first got sick.

On June 10th I am getting a blood test. That blood test is supposed to tell me if Oregon is making me sick. I mean, I felt good in both South Carolina and Colorado. So what if there is some, you know, mold or something that I'm allergic to? One that only grows here?

There is no right answer. Who wants to be allergic to the place they live? And yet, if it promises excitement, that is what I am wishing for in my heart. There are things I don't understand, and this is one of them.

It is nice to know, though, that God knows what is going to happen and why it's going to happen. And that whatever happens I can know it was the best thing. Or at least the right thing. The thing that was supposed to happen.

Holding My Hand

I GOT BLOOD DRAWN again yesterday. As the doctor prepared the vials for the blood and the big ugly needle and all those sorts of things, my mom looked at me and said, "Do you want me to hold your hand?"

"Yes," I said, like I always do.

About halfway through the filling of the second vial, the doctor made some sort of comment that I just wanted a hand massage, and I really didn't need my mom to hold my hand at all. I was a very brave girl, he said.

Yeah, yeah, doctors are supposed to say things like that. But seriously, I normally shrink away from touchy-feely things, and getting blood drawn doesn't really hurt very badly.

The thing about getting blood drawn, I realized, is that I hate the idea of it more than I hate the pain of it. Yeah, it hurts somewhat, but it's a pain I can stand. Because even if it doesn't really hurt, you can still feel that needle there, poking into you. And if you happen to look at it, even if you try your hardest not to, you can see that vial slowly filling with blood. Your blood. Something about knowing that gives me the chills and makes me want my hand held.

I'm not sure why I needed three vials of blood just to see if I'm allergic to Oregon, but that's what he took.

I Wish . . .

I WISH I COULD GO somewhere far away and meet someone new and do something exciting, even if it hurt.

I wish I could magically find a place to put everything.

I wish I could figure skate.

I wish bugs would sense my presence and flee. I saw a moth in the Honda today. I screamed, and Amy got scared. It died very easily. Then I came home and there were little bugs on the toilet paper. Ugh.

I wish everybody would say "pol-ka dots" instead of "poke-a dots."

I wish I would never accidentally be rude.

I wish I could wear costumes everywhere without being embarrassed.

I wish the doctor would just call and make an appointment for me to come see my test results already. I don't like waiting.

Tea Party

TODAY I WAS INVITED TO a tea. I love tea. I love dressing up. I don't understand why people stop dressing up and having tea parties when they grow up.

So I was all decked out in a silky pink dress, a floppy pink hat, white gloves, silver shoes, the whole nine yards. The other girls came dressed normally, and then changed into old bridesmaid dresses there.

We all sat around a beautifully decorated table and chatted about the dashing princes of our acquaintance.

We went on a walk, then, in all our fluffy pink attire. It was great to see people's expressions when they drove past us, and we all waved to them.

Dressing up, pretending, and drinking tea. What better way to spend your time? Unfortunately, it seemed to exhaust me a great deal, and, though there was a sleepover tonight that I was invited to, I did not attend.

No Go

I HAVE THIS LITTLE sick feeling growing in the pit of my stomach. And I am also feeling frustrated. And mad.

I am not going to the BMA Convention in South Carolina. I am upset. I really, really, really wanted to go. I was counting on going. Because I am longing for adventure, and I wanted to see Mitch again.

And there is more to it than that. I thought maybe if I went back to South Carolina I would feel well again. I want to feel well so badly.

But no, I need to stay home and watch over things here. Sigh.

Lists

FIVE THINGS I DON'T understand about life:

1. Why everyone always seems to be bored and/or dissatisfied with their life.
2. Why you have to add sugar to applesauce but not apple cider, even though they are both made by just squishing apples.
3. Why people don't like to read.
4. Why I'm still sick.
5. Why I can only think of four things right now even though I'm always thinking of things I don't understand about life.

Five things I've learned because of my sickness:

1. No matter how many blood tests I take, they're all going to come out negative.

2. It's easier to lie when random people ask, "How are you?" than it is to explain the truth.

3. The whole idea that "God is never going to give you more than you can handle" is silly because you can handle anything if you are forced to.

4. I am going to be sick forever.

5. No matter how bad it gets it could always get worse, but somehow that thought isn't comforting in the slightest.

Five things I wish I was able to do:

1. Like every type of food.

2. Always have something clever to say.

3. Not be afraid to do things unless they are actually dangerous (like jumping off a cliff or swimming with sharks).

4. Read slow-moving classics without getting bored.

5. Make the most of life, despite my illness.

Five things I wish I had:

1. Picture frames to fit all my lovely fairy tale pictures.

2. Better video editing software.

3. A place in my room to set my dressmaker's dummy, which I got for graduation.

4. Magic potion.

5. Some of that BBQ pork from that Chinese restaurant in Junction City—the place with the really gross water and the waitress who gives out back rubs.

Five weird things I've fallen in love with in a dream (or at least had a crush on):

1. A bird that was sometimes called a firebird and sometimes called a snowbird.

2. John Travolta's character in the movie *Grease* (I don't remember his name, probably due to the fact that I've never even seen the movie. Just read about it.).

3. This guy who was in this Christian band that had one song called "Eva Was a Mermaid." Only each time they sang it they made Eva a different thing (such as, "Eva was a cheeseburger," or "Eva was a mouse."). He also worked in a mechanical pencil factory.

4. This guy who controlled (and lived in) the clouds, had really powerful black hands, wore silver earrings that were actually little scissors, and reattached his hand to his arm after it came off when I tried to climb up to the clouds with a rope tied around his wrist.

5. A clothespin.

Manderly

MOM AND I WENT "shopping" for bedroom furniture, checking out stuff we'd seen on Craigslist. I've always secretly, in the innermost depths of my heart, wanted a canopy bed. Well what do you know, some girl decided her canopy bed was too babyish for her a couple weeks after she started sleeping in it. She's getting a new bed, her dad told us, complete with Hannah Montana sheets.

Hmm . . . I wonder how long it will be until the bed becomes too babyish for me, and I beg for a new bed and some Hannah Montana sheets.

I named my bedroom "Manderly." I got the name from the book *Rebecca,* which is an amazing book. Only I spell it "Manderly" instead of "Manderley" because when I printed the sign for the door, I didn't realize it was spelled with an extra *e*.

Manderly will be a lovely paradise. I am currently in the process of moving in.

I have so much stuff it's crazy.

Staying Home

THERE IS A SMALL TOWN called Winston a couple of hours away. There is a little Mennonite church in the town of Winston, and every year they have a Vacation Bible School for the kids in town. Lots of kids come. The church is small. They need help. So last year Amy, Stephy, and I went to Winston for a week to help out. I can't even describe how much fun it was.

They're going again this year of course. They are but not me, and somehow that really hurts.

Not only that, but my family is taking a canoe trip again this summer. It's an annual thing. Matt and Mom aren't interested, but the rest of us like to go. We swim, camp, and paddle down the beautiful Willamette River. It is beyond lovely.

Canoeing is sort of my thing. No one else in my family can paddle a canoe as well as I can, except for Dad of course, and maybe Matt, but Matt lost interest in canoeing a while ago.

This is the way it usually is for me: I can spend all day learning to do something, like skateboarding, or playing a video game, or using a pogo stick, and Amy or Ben or Steven will come along and, in five minutes, be better at it than me. But canoeing is different. Canoeing is my thing.

And besides, there is nothing more lovely than paddling down the river at dusk, laughing with your siblings, and smelling the unbelievably beautiful smell of the river.

By now you may have guessed that my weak little arms can't paddle a canoe, and my weak little self can't sit in a canoe all day with no place to rest my head. You may have guessed that missing Winston, the canoe trip, and the BMA convention has me feeling much like I felt last March when I couldn't go to Eagle Crest or Kenya. And your guesses are right. That is exactly how I feel.

Only there is one more thing. The doctor called. I am not allergic to Oregon. So all my distant dreams of moving somewhere else, and meeting people and getting better, are dashed to pieces.

Good Lives

SOMETIMES I THINK my life is pretty good. I have a new, big-but-not-too-big room filled with wonderful fascinating things. I have a canopy bed. I have my own computer, my own video camera, my own dress form. Sure, I don't have a lot of money, but I don't have anything to buy, and I never go shopping anyway. Everybody keeps giving me wonderful things.

Everyday I wake up in my beautiful canopy bed, with a satin bedspread covering me and a fuzzy orange pillow under my head. Sitting on a tray by my bed, there is always breakfast and Kenyan tea prepared by my dear mother.

I can sleep in as late as I want. I can go to bed as late as I want. I don't have to help with many chores, and if I am working and don't feel well because of it, Mom or Amy will usually be lenient. If I ask someone to do something for me, they will usually do it. I can read books or surf the Internet or watch movies or hang out with my cool, interesting family. I can write stories or read stuff I've written years ago or go into my amazing closet and become any character I feel like being.

Sure I feel sick all the time, but if I'm not really doing anything, it's easy to ignore it, and life just goes rolling right along.

In other words, I have a very easy life.

But sometimes, I visit random blogs and see people who, in their "about me" section, write "I am just one of the 'runners' in this crazy race we call life!"

Or "I love life and making new friends."

Or "I'm on the ride of my life and am hanging on for dear life!"

Or I go on Facebook, and my friends' status updates say things like "Susie Smith is aching from a long day at work . . ." or "Jessica Miller is going to the lake."

Or I go on virtually any young person's blog and read, "Sorry I haven't written in so long, I've been so busy . . ."

In those moments, that's when I tend to get jealous and hate my easy life.

If you would have asked me a year ago if I wanted a normal life, I would have said, "No way!" But back then I wanted an extraordinary life, not what I've got.

Now I just want a normal teenage life. I want to ache from a long day at work. I want to be so busy that I don't have time to post on my blog. I want to be on the ride of my life, you know?

I feel like someday I'm going to wake up and realize, *You know what, I've never really done anything in life. Why haven't I ever done anything in life?*

Sometimes I forget what it's like not to be sick.

Eighteen

I AM GOING CRAZY. I don't want to see anyone. I don't want to talk to anyone. All I want to do is lie on the floor and thrash around and make it all go away.

Today is my birthday. I feel horrible. I wish I could say it's the worst birthday of my life but it isn't. My worst birthday was the one I spent in the funeral home two years ago, when my cousin Lenny committed suicide. This is just a plain old horrible birthday.

I am eighteen but I don't believe I am eighteen. I can't make myself believe it. When my grandpa died I didn't believe he was dead until I saw him in the casket. I knew it but didn't believe it. That is how it is now.

How come I keep thinking about people I loved who died? Why don't I believe I am eighteen?

I don't want to be eighteen! Why? Because I was never seventeen. All I ever was, was sick. My last year of school, my last year of being dependent on my parents, my last year of being a kid, and I never got any of it. Now it's gone and I don't want it to be gone. I want it to come back.

I just decided that seventeen is the perfect age to be and I want to be seventeen forever.

I feel so horribly sick. I don't want to talk to anyone. I want to pull the covers over my head and make it all go away.

Allergies

YESTERDAY, A WEEK AFTER my horrible birthday, I woke up feeling odd. Oddly good. Not even close to totally better or anything, but good enough that it felt odd.

Wednesday, I'm getting lots of blood sucked out of my arm. When I was twelve, Dr. Hanson gave me a blood test, and figured out what foods I was allergic to. I still don't eat those foods, even though I probably got over those allergies.

After the blood test results come in, I may be able to eat chicken or cranberries or goat cheese again, but I also may find new things I'm allergic to. Still, I think I might like to have new things to be allergic to just to mix things up a little. Then again, I sort of lost my taste for apples and oranges and ice cream, and I never did like olives or goat milk or tin. Who eats tin anyway?

Ha! That reminds me, once my friend Preston told me

that he and Justin figured out why I was so sick. Their theory was that I was building a tin shed and got really hungry.

But I would love to eat chicken and drink cranberry juice again.

Something Happy For Once

WELL . . . I WENT to the doctor and they stuck a needle in my arm, and lots of blood pumped through the needle and through a little tube and into these glass vials, and Mom held my hand and joked about how this is the one time she gets to hold my hand, yadda yadda yadda.

After that was all taken care of, and there was a cotton ball and a Band-Aid on my arm, Mom asked the doctor if there was anything she should know about the results from the previous blood test I had taken.

The doctor looked over my records and informed us that, when I got tested way back in November, my West Nile count was 57. When I got the last blood test, on June 10, it was 39. Normal is 30.

Okay, yeah, I was a little confused about what exactly those numbers mean, but I got the gist of it.

I am officially getting better.

It was very, very encouraging. He said that if I was tested again in six months he would almost be positive it would all be gone. I could have cried for joy.

I want to go to Bible School next year. Oh, and Kenya? Is it possible that I'll be able to go to Kenya too? My family is thinking about going around Christmas, you know, and if I could go along . . .

Of course Kenya and Bible School are months ahead, but honestly, this is the first time I've actually thought I might be well enough to go both places. I don't know, I just seriously think sometimes that I'm gonna be sick forever.

Somehow, the idea that I could still have months of sickness ahead of me doesn't bother me. Just so I can get well. I just want to know that I'm actually gonna get well.

The doctor also seemed to think that once I have an update on what foods I'm allergic to, that will help me feel better and get well faster. I certainly hope so. That would be amazing.

Lovely Thoughts and Things

MY LIFE HAS BEEN just right recently, and not just right as in perfect but just right as in right now, at this recovering stage.

And yes, it appears I am recovering. I keep having good days, pretty much ever since that Sunday I woke up feeling oddly good. I hang around, drinking tea and writing and just enjoying being in Manderly. It's nice, really, loving your room.

I don't go many places and do many things, mostly because harvest is on and everyone is working, but I like the whole thing of just being calm in a beautiful place while I dream of Bible School and Kenya.

I wonder what percentage of songs are about love.

The color silver is just shiny gray, but is gold shiny yellow or shiny brown? I asked Jenny that and she said that gold was shiny yellow. I argued with her, and then she said gold was shiny tan. But that was kind of silly because when I had said "brown" I was thinking "light brown," which is pretty much the same as tan.

My cousin Jessi just came over to chat with me. It was a lot of fun. I made her some tea. I wish more people would just come visit me randomly and I would make them tea.

I like my life right now.

Wake-Up Call

TODAY WAS SUPPOSED TO be the day when I would go in and get the results of my blood test, but in typical Emily fashion, the blood test "didn't work."

This morning Mom came into my room with my tea. "Are you awake enough for me to talk to you about something?" she asked.

I grunted.

She looked around the room, fiddled with this, fiddled with that, looked up, looked down . . . I wanted to scream. I have this weird pet peeve about people doing that, but have you ever noticed that when you have just woken up, your pet peeves turn into something more like torture? I couldn't stand it. "What are you doing?" I asked her.

"Looking for your sugar and a spoon, so you can drink your tea, so you'll be awake enough to talk."

Oh great.

"Just talk to me now," I said.

"Okay." She sat down. "It turns out the reason the blood test didn't work is because your white blood cells died out too quickly!"

"What does that mean?" I asked.

"I don't know," said Mom. Then she went on and on about how she looked up all this stuff online and she e-mailed Aunt Barb, who is a doctor. Mom was all worried because she was going on a trip and wouldn't be able to talk to Dr. Hanson about my poor white blood cells very soon.

"Why can't we just wait until you get back and then talk to Dr. Hanson?" I asked. "It's not like I'm dying or anything."

She gave me this look of astonishment and then laughed. "I never even thought of that," she said.

But she's still worried anyway, even though both Dr. Hanson and I told her not to worry.

August 2008

Saturday Cleaning

IF I WAS AT THE BMA Convention with my mom and Amy, I would have something of substance to write about. As it is, I am stuck home with the daunting task of keeping the whole house in order. Hello? I have trouble just keeping Manderly in order!

And, as today is Saturday cleaning, there's a good deal of vacuuming and washing and sweeping and dusting going on. And even worse, I need to try to motivate siblings.

Oh! I do have one thing to say. The other day I did something I never before realized I could do.

It started when I was looking at some flyers for the store Fred Meyer. There were these short little vests, and I couldn't decide if they were cute or weird. They were the sort of thing I might buy if they were for two dollars at Goodwill, but not twenty dollars at Fred Meyer.

Then I got a crazy idea.

I started pinning newspapers to my dressmaker's dummy, and made myself a pattern for a short vest. Then I found some black denim on the shelf of fabric that I'm allowed to use without asking, cut out the pieces, and sewed them together. I now have a cute little vest that fits me perfectly!

Now before you start thinking I'm some amazing seamstress, I must admit that I had to sew the whole thing with the serger because I couldn't get the bobbin in the sewing machine correctly, and Mom couldn't help me, of course, being gone. Furthermore, since I wasn't sure how to put seam allowances in a pattern, I just traced around the pattern with chalk and cut an approximate half-inch around that. I was planning on following the inside edge of the chalk with the sewing machine needle, which would probably have worked, but unfortunately that is difficult to do with a serger. As a result, I had trouble getting things to match up.

But I totally love it, even if one strap is a little wider than the other.

Stinkerbell

I WANT TO GO to BMA Bible Institute so badly. A year and a half ago Amy went, and the year before that Matt went. Both of them had incredibly good times. I am old enough now, and if I can just get my schoolwork done, get my diploma signed, and get well, I can go. Doctor Hanson says I'm getting better, plus I have been having good days ever since that Sunday in the middle of July I woke up feeling oddly good.

Of course there is the tuition factor, which is getting paid partially by the church and partially by my parents, but some of it I have to earn myself. Seeing as how I'm too sick to have a job, I have to resort to other means.

Enter Stinkerbell.

Stinkerbell is a character I made up, a fairy who stinks and tends to shed a lot of pixie dust. Orlis Avery is a garbage truck driver. I made up a story about them, painted pictures to go along with it, and spent hours on the computer making it into a little book. Mom took several copies to the fair with her when she went to sell her book, and nearly every one sold.

Yay!

I also wrote a story for these Sunday school papers our church gets. They accept almost anything according to my mom, and they pay well. I've sold them a couple of stories before, but as a general rule, I would much rather be writing stores about fairies drinking coffee than children learning lessons.

But like I said, they pay, and I need money.

Morning Person

EVERY MORNING I get up and drink my tea and sit at my window seat and watch people ride bikes or drive cars below my window. I get lots of stuff done then. Lots of schoolwork.

Then I get tired and am tired for the rest of the day. If I take a nap I will get enough energy to perhaps take a walk in the rain, and then I will be tired again.

It's odd to find yourself go from a night person to a morning person.

Ten More Random Facts About Me

1. I'm scared to look in the mirror when it's dark. It always feels like something horrible and freaky will look back at me.
2. I have a wart on the second toe of my right foot.
3. When I was little, I used to think high notes were low notes and low notes were high notes. When I took piano lessons I was very confused. (I didn't take lessons for very long.)

4. If someone gives me something and I hate it, I feel horrible, so I usually try to pretend it's magic, and then I can make myself love it.

5. If I was like Jerry Spinelli's *Stargirl* and didn't care a hoot if people thought my clothes were weird, I would wear costumes all the time—pretty costumes, not Santa Claus costumes or anything.

6. I have a habit of imagining amazing stories in my head, but when I write them down I realize that they have virtually no plot. It is very frustrating.

7. I used to write a random fact about me on every blog post, but then I realized they all had to do with food. Like how I don't like eggs except for the yolk of soft-boiled eggs, or how I like to eat pie dough, or the way I like mustard but not ketchup, or tea but not coffee. It was embarrassing. So I stopped putting a random fact about myself on every blog post.

8. I have two pink hats. I am wearing the one I got for my graduation right now. I got my other pink hat in Mexico. As soon as I put it on my head, I knew it was just right.

9. I've always wondered what it would feel like to faint.

10. I have a stuffed frog named Professor Dough-Head.

The Results

APPARENTLY I AM ALLERGIC to caffeine and cane sugar. What? No more lovely black tea in the morning? With sugar? I suppose now I can eat apples and oranges and cranberries and poppy seeds and carrageenan gum and even goat cheese, but still . . .

Cane sugar is in everything. Seriously. Tortillas, clam chowder, you name it. Everywhere I go, I have to read labels. It's a good thing I'm sick and don't often go to friends' houses or out to eat because what would I do then?

And caffeine, I mean, I'm tired enough as it is.

I'm also still allergic to chicken and some other things with odd sounding names. Like dibutyl phthalate. I mean, what is that anyway?

One more thing. I have now been sick for an entire year. I'm glad I didn't know it would last a year when I first got sick.

Application Fee

THINGS WERE GOING SO GOOD. The doctor predicted I would be well in time to go to Bible School, and my parents and I figured out a way I could actually conceivably do it, financially and all. First term would start just after Christmas, and I would go with Amy, Bethany, J. D., and Brandon. But I would go second term too, and the other people from my church would go home. Just me against the world.

Suddenly, I had a renewed ambition to get my schoolwork done, because I obviously can't go to Bible School without a high school diploma. And even though my life was boring, I could stand it, just dreaming of what was to come.

I filled out the forms that were for me to fill out, and gave reference forms to different people I knew. Everything was ready. I carefully sealed the envelope and proceeded to the mailbox. The whole world seemed full of promise.

But wait! I had forgotten the stamp. Back inside I went, rummaging around in the office.

"Do you have a check in there?" Mom asked.

Oh, duh. The application fee, $150 per term. "I forgot," I said. "Can you make out a $300 check?"

Mom was hesitant. "I don't really feel comfortable putting a $300 nonrefundable check in there without asking your dad first," she said.

"But Dad already said he'd pay the application fee!" I said, starting to panic. It felt as though my dream of going to Bible Institute in 2009 would vanish before my eyes if I didn't get that check in the mail in five minutes. But my earnest begging and pleading amounted to nothing.

It turned out that Dad thought the entire application fee was $150. So he had to e-mail the headmaster and ask if I could have the application fee for second term be refundable if I felt too sick to go.

By the time the headmaster replied, I realized that there is no way I can know, now, where I'm gonna be in January. Who can know if I'll be better or not? There is no guarantee. I could be sick forever. I am not going to Bible School, and I am terribly depressed about it.

Why I Feel Depressed Today

1. I didn't get much sleep last night because there was a moth in my room that wouldn't die.

2. I had a horrible dream that made me wake up feeling sickish.

3. I spent all morning cramming on schoolwork since I've been slacking off, on account of not having any Bible School motivation.

4. I am still far behind on schoolwork.

5. Remember the story I sent to the Sunday school papers our church gets? Well they rejected it. The rejection slip said, "Thank you, but I do not need this story."

What does that mean, anyway? That my story was horrible but they want to let me down easy, or that they have enough stories and don't need anymore, thereby ending my get-rich-quick-by-writing-stupid-stories plan?

6. I worked on a Xanga message off and on all day and then somehow erased it.

7. Facebook acted all weird and goofy today.

8. My room went from being a little messy to a huge mess.

9. I am not going to Bible School.

10. I can't have caffeine or cane sugar.

The Day I Would Just as Soon Forget

THEY ALL WENT TO Justin and Stephy's house to play volleyball. Not me. I was sick with sadness and depression.

I lay in Manderly all alone. *You can't let it beat you,* I told myself. So I took a shower and dressed in a funky outfit and started walking to Stephy's.

I saw the youth group in the yard playing volleyball. But just as soon as I sat down to watch and catch my breath, they were done, and standing around talking. I went over to stand around and talk with them.

"Shall we do something?" they asked each other. "We could, you know, go out to eat."

Going out to eat seemed a good plan to them. Not to me, of course, but I wasn't about to spoil their fun. They discussed where they would go and what vehicles they would ride in. I tried to swallow the lump in my throat, but it just got bigger.

What was I supposed to do, go and drink water? Send the waitress back into the kitchen countless times to see if certain foods had sugar in them? Is this stupid sugar thing going to ruin my life? I started walking home. I burst into tears.

Halfway through the first field I saw headlights, and my friend Lyndon's blue rig bouncing through the field. He stopped in front of me and rolled down his window. "Want a ride?" he asked.

It was pretty much dark already. I squeezed in along with all the other people Lyndon was taking to whatever restaurant they had decided on. I just sat there, staring out the window, tears streaming down my face. It was embarrassing, but I didn't even care anymore.

"Do you want me to take you home?" Lyndon asked.

"Yes please," I said.

Now I'm alone in Manderly again. And I wish I could just forget today, you know?

A Job

I GOT A JOB, SORT OF, driving our van full of kids home from school every day, and dropping them off at their houses. I also have to help out in the classroom some. Since there were a lot of students who had things they needed to read out loud today, I spent a good deal of time there listening to them read.

Josh is one of the younger kids, and he cracks me up so badly. He had a bit of a hard time reading, but acted like he really wanted to learn. He paused in the middle of the passage he was reading and said, "How about you read a word and then I read a word? That's what my mom does."

"I would," I said, "except it wouldn't be fair, because all the other kids have to read everything."

Then he started fake crying, so I started fake crying too . . . "Boo hoo! I just want to be fair!"

He laughed and laughed, and then sat up straight and finished reading the page without a problem.

Later, in a story we were reading, there was a character named Ace talking to Baba, his pet lamb. Every time Josh came to the letter *I* he thought it was *L*.

"No," I kept explaining, "it's *I*, not *L*, because sometimes they leave the little marks off the top and the bottom."

"There are lots of *I*'s," he said. "I want to count the *I*'s."

So he counted them and then started reading again. I think there were ten.

Soon he came to another *I* and again thought it was an *L*. When I explained it to him again, he said, "Bike. Is bike an *I* word? Can you say some *I* words?"

So I said "dike" and "spike," and he laughed. "Let's say some *I* words every time we come to an *I*," he said. But then it was break time.

The whole ordeal wore me out terribly, though. I came home and took a four-hour nap.

Unfortunately, as a whole, life still feels pretty pointless. I mean, I have nothing to look forward to. I guess I should just be glad I have a job and good days. That's what I wanted, right?

But there is nothing new on the horizon at all. Even our Christmas/Kenya plans seem to be backfiring.

Just Ask

TODAY I PRAYED WHILE taking a shower in the dark, and that's when I decided something. I need to talk to my dad about this. I have no inspiration to do my schoolwork anymore . . . no inspiration to make money, really, and no inspiration to go through life happily, because all I have to look forward to is endless bleakness.

I've told my mom about this before and she feels sorry for me. But my dad is more of an answer man.

If I do my schoolwork and try to pay half, is there any way I could go on a vacation somewhere?

Please?

I just need something to look forward to.

I must ask him. He can make things better, but he can't make things worse.

Not Living

TODAY WAS A HORRIBLE BEYOND HORRIBLE day in terms of how I felt physically.

My cousin Justin got video chat on Instant Messenger. I've never video chatted before in my life and it was fun, only we couldn't actually talk to each other . . . just see each other.

I am not living life anymore. I am dreaming it. I am so sick everything is like a dream. Who in real life would do a video chat without sound and be beyond amazed?

I don't know what to do now because I know I can't sleep and I am so hot and miserable, and, if you can believe it, still trying to wrap my mind around the wonders of video chat.

I can't read. It hurts my head. I could watch movies endlessly, but hey, that is what I was doing, and I can't do that all night because, seriously, that would be pretty crazy.

I never did talk to my dad because I got so sick and you can't talk things through in a rational undreamlike manner if you are crazy sick.

I spent a good deal of time today trying to rationalize what keeps trains from running into each other.

Dad

STILL CRAZY SICK.

Oh, I talked to Dad today despite my horrid sickness. He was beyond amazing, and approached it with all his problem-solving skills. I was crying and carrying on like a crazy person because I am sort of, well, crazy right now, and he made all these plans. And I might go somewhere someday . . . like Kansas to see the famous Mast family or something. I am so relieved. I have something to live for now, so that is amazing. I should have talked to Dad about that problem ages ago.

Everything is not so hopeless after all.

The Shower

I HAD A LOVELY SHOWER in the dark and was sitting on the floor (still in the dark) thinking about guys who hate cats, and the door started to open. Like someone's coming in!

I screamed. Loud. Gut reaction, hello?

Oh yeah, did I mention it was three in the morning?

It was Matt. He wanted to turn off the fan, and my scream totally freaked him out. He didn't think anyone was in there, you know, since the light was off.

Helminthosporium

HELMINTHOSPORIUM SATIVUM is currently voted "most likely to rock my little world." I didn't even know what it was when it showed up on my allergy test along with cane sugar and caffeine and whatnot. So I just sort of ignored it.

It's a major reaction though. The others—cane sugar, chicken, locust bean gum, whatever—they are all minor reactions. So Mom has been doing research on helminthosporium.

Turns out that it is some mold that grows on grass in mild wet climates. Well, what place has more grass and mild wet climates than here? The main crop is grass for Pete's sake!

I don't know why this *helminthosporium sativum* didn't show up when I got tested to see if I was allergic to Oregon. But if this brings me excitement and wellness, I'll take it. I really like the idea of moving and then getting better. I always have.

The Coast

I DECIDED TO GO TO the coast with my older Smucker cousins. I still feel horrible. But all I was doing all day was watching movies and knitting. Everything else was hurting my head. It's beginning to feel like I live in a movie instead of in real life. So maybe a change of pace will be good for me.

Everyone is having so much fun. Everyone but me. I lie upstairs in bed watching movies or knitting like always. Sometimes I make my way downstairs and try to find something to eat, something I can have. It is terribly, terribly hard.

I haven't gone to the beach yet. I probably won't at all. I am too sick. I can barely make it up the stairs sometimes.

People talk to me. That is fun. It makes me laugh.

Then I lie in the dark, hearing everyone else laughing and having fun, and I feel so absolutely alone. That's when I cry.

It is so much easier to have no life when I'm alone in Manderly. It's so much harder when I can hear the laughter and none of it is mine.

I wonder if the good points of this trip will outweigh the bad—if it is worth it to laugh if I am also going to cry.

More Helminthosporium

HELMINTHOSPORIUM SATIVUM. That's what we talk about these days. Where could I go to get away from it? Will I get better if I get away? How can we know?

I want to get away so badly. I want to have an adventure and get better. I don't want to leave my beloved Manderly forever, but I would rather have wellness than Manderly. No question.

October 2008

Redmond

IT IS 3:16 AM, and for the life of me I cannot get to sleep. Under normal circumstances, this would not bother me. I would just read or write or twiddle my thumbs until I did fall into restful slumber, and sleep in as late as I wanted the next morning. But as it is, I am currently sharing a hotel room with my parents, and they are both sound asleep. I tried reading with my cell phone for light until I ran out of battery. I tried going to sleep several times but it never worked. Now I am trying to type while sitting in the bathroom so the light and tapping sounds won't wake up my parents.

We are in Redmond, Oregon.

I am hungry. So dreadfully hungry. I could eat an apple, but even though I am apparently over my apple allergy, home-grown apples still tend to give me stomachaches. I could eat Saltine crackers with peanut butter, but how messy would that be? In the dark and all? And plain Saltine crackers are drier than dry, and I am already feeling dry. My eyes are dry. My lips are dry. The inside of my nose is dry. There is no wetness here in eastern Oregon like there is in the valley.

Tomorrow we are going to look at apartments. I may move here.

This bathroom floor is not a comfortable place to sit. Maybe I'll sit in the bathtub. Ah, much better. Yes, I am sitting in a bathtub in a hotel in Redmond writing at 3:30 AM. That sounds very interesting. The thought makes me a little happier.

I want to get better so badly. You have no idea how badly. I can hardly imagine myself better. I remember a time I played volleyball over and over, or a time I partied all night and how much fun I had, and I think, *How could I do that? Didn't I get tired? Didn't I get a headache? What was it like to feel so wonderful all the time?*

I need my sleep. I can't drink caffeine so I am bound to be tired tomorrow.

Ten Reasons Why I Am Moving to Redmond

1. Redmond is one of the driest cities in Oregon. If there is no moisture, helminthosporium can't grow.
2. If helminthosporium can't grow, my terrible immune system can improve.

3. If my terrible immune system improves, perhaps I will finally be able to push West Nile from my system.

4. Redmond is only two-and-a-half hours from home, so someone in my family or one of my friends should usually be able to stay with me.

5. After an extremely annoying wild goose chase involving a studio apartment, an office in a closet under some stairs in an obscure building in Bend, and weird complications involving the fact that I am living in the apartment but Dad is paying, we finally found a suitable place. It's safe. It's close to important things like the library. It has a bathroom, a kitchen and living room, and a bedroom. Plus it has beautiful windows.

6. I need adventure. I need something new. I've wanted it ever since I first got sick. Actually, I've always wanted it. But not desperately like while I've been sick.

7. The sky is beautiful. Well, okay, technically that played no part in deciding to move, but it is definitely an added bonus. I mean, I knew western Oregon was wet and eastern Oregon was dry, but I never made the connection in my head that dry equals beautiful cloudless sky.

8. There is a good Mennonite church a half hour away that I can go to. The people there are so nice and

welcoming. Unfortunately, there isn't a youth group. But it is still a great church.

9. I need to be tested, you know? Because while I am convinced that moving here will make me better, based on things like South Carolina and going to Colorado for the wedding and feeling better in the dry summer months, Dad is still a tad bit skeptical. He wants to see if I improve over several months and then arrange for a more permanent place to live.

There is no tenth reason. If there is I can't think if it. But it looks dumb to talk about nine reasons for something.

10. I thought of another reason! Redmond was founded on my birthday.

Okay, that was a pretty lame reason.

Wide Awake

I'VE BEEN DOING SOME weird half-sleep thing for the past five-and-a-half hours, and now I'm awake and tired and hot and stressed out because I have a gazillion more things I need to pack before I leave in twelve hours. I am so hungry. My head hurts so badly. I am wide awake. I don't know what to do. It's one in the morning.

A New View

I'M HERE, SITTING AT my new window, looking out over Redmond, my new home. It is lovely outside. The sky is dusty blue, and there are pink clouds.

I love this window. What will my life be like while this is my window, my view of the world? What will happen to me? Will I be happy? Will I be sad?

I don't know. I haven't the faintest clue what the future holds, and I love every minute of it. Anything could happen! Anything but lying on my old bed in my old house facing the same thing day after day like I have for the past year.

Do you understand what I'm saying?

There is hope.

Epilogue

I have a job.

I have a cute little motor scooter to get places on.

My new window and view of the world is in the tower room of a very old Victorian house in Colorado.

And while some would look at the above statements and say, "Yay! It worked! She is all better, and now she has a perfect life," the truth is, I am not all better. But I am some better. And Redmond did work.

Unfortunately, while Redmond did amazing things for my health, there were things it lacked, too. For instance, as it turned out, the Mennonite church was far away enough that it was too hard for me to build relationships with the people there and really feel like a part of the church. In Redmond, I also had to do without a youth group to hang out with and a place to serve. Colorado has all those things, plus a dry, helminthosporium-free climate. It also is the home of a family that has been friends with our family for ages. They treat me like I belong to their family, since I am so far from my own.

The Mennonites out here have a mission: raising babies born to ladies in prison. When the mother is released, the baby is given back to her. If it weren't for the mission, the babies would go into foster care, and the mothers would never be able to get their babies back. I find it so beautiful and self-sacrificial.

The mission also runs a couple thrift stores that help support the mission, and they gave me a job at one of them. A job with a totally flexible schedule. If I feel icky I can go straight home. If I feel great I can work a couple more hours. It is amazing. Totally amazing.

All I can say is that somehow it all worked out.

And every day I get a little bit better.

Book Club Discussion Questions for EMILY

1. Much of *Emily* is based on the author's blog, which she writes primarily for friends and family. What did you find unique or interesting about Emily's writing style and voice throughout the book?

2. Emily is a Mennonite, and her religious affiliation is a big part of who she is as a person. What kinds of things did you notice in Emily's social, school, and family life that reflect her Mennonite background? How do these things differ from your own experience? How are they the same?

3. How do you think Emily's overall outlook on life is based on the way she handled the challenges of West Nile?

4. Put yourself in Emily's shoes. How would you feel if you were diagnosed with a rare and incurable sickness such as West Nile? Who would you turn to for help? How would you cope?

5. Emily goes to a Mennonite school with thirty-two students. How do you think the social scene would differ at a school this size versus your school? Do you think it would be easier or more difficult socially to attend such a small school as compared to a more typical-sized high school?

6. When Emily is at her lowest point and is feeling like life is hopeless, she often turns to God for comfort. Have you ever felt this way? What kinds of things do you do to find comfort and solace when you're struggling with feelings of hopelessness?

7. *Emily* takes place over the course of a year and a half. Did you notice any changes in Emily's maturity and perspective as the story progressed?

8. Emily shares her unique quirkiness through her writing, such as her habit of naming inanimate objects. If you were to write a memoir of your life, what quirky things would the reader discover about you?

9. Did you learn any surprising or interesting facts in the course of reading this book?

10. Is *Emily* a story of hope? Why or why not?